SACRED RHYTHMS

SACRED RHYTHMS

FINDING A PEACEFUL PACE
IN A HECTIC WORLD

CHRISTINE SINE, M.D.

Baker Books

A Division of Baker Book House Co
Grand Rapids, Michigan 49516

© 2003 by Christine Sine

Published by Baker Books
a division of Baker Book House Company
P.O. Box 6287, Grand Rapids, MI 49516-6287
www.bakerbooks.com

Printed in the United States of America

Library of Congress Cataloging-in-Publication Data
Aroney-Sine, Christine.
    Sacred rhythms : finding a peaceful pace in a hectic world / Christine
Sine.
        p.   cm.
    Includes bibliographical references.
    ISBN 0-8010-6414-7 (pbk.)
    1. Peace of mind—Religious aspects—Christianity. 2. Rhythm—Religious
aspects—Christianity. 3. Church year. I. Title.
BV908.5.A76 2003
248.4—dc21   2003012188

CONTENTS

ACKNOWLEDGMENTS

*W*riting a book is never the work of a single person. This book is no exception. So many have contributed stories and shared with me their own struggles to develop a sacred rhythm in the midst of their hectic lives. I am extremely grateful for the friends who have encouraged me and helped me keep my own life rhythm balanced throughout this process. I would particularly like to thank the members of our small group—Janet and Coe Hutchison, Don and Patty Doty, and Stan Thornburg—and my close friends Cheryl Mackey and Ruth Austin.

I would especially like to thank our assistants at Mustard Seed Associates, Valerie Norwood and Aimee Buchholz, who have made it possible for me to free up time to work on this project. I also am grateful for the input of Tom Balke, Eydie Cowley, and Ev and Gary Heard, who took time to read along as I completed each chapter and gave me their very helpful advice. Finally, I would like to express my appreciation and gratitude for my husband, Tom, who encouraged me to write this book. Without his loving support it never would have been completed.

INTRODUCTION

*A*imee sat on the edge of her chair, fuming. The Saturday evening service at Friends Memorial Church in Seattle was not going as she had expected, and she couldn't focus on God.

The service began with a few moments of silence.

Then Heather started to read, "Hear, O Lord, when I cry aloud, be gracious to me and answer me—"

Suddenly the strident tones of a cell phone pierced the tranquil atmosphere, totally disrupting Aimee's serenity.

The woman apologized profusely, and Heather started afresh. She had hardly opened her mouth when the phone rang again.

The woman hurriedly whispered into the phone and ended the conversation.

Heather continued, "My heart says to thee, 'Thy face Lord do I seek. . . .'"

The phone rang yet again.

This time the woman carried on a conversation in a voice loud enough to drown out the Scripture reading.

By now the whole congregation was in a state of shock and obviously upset at the constant interruptions. Suddenly a strobe light flashed on. Its garish light jangled Aimee's already frayed nerves.

Over the next few minutes a radio, a TV, and a stereo started playing. Aimee heard someone vacuuming out in the corridor, adding to the noise and chaos. By now Aimee knew that this was a setup, but she wasn't sure where to focus.

Heather shouted above the din, "In my deepest being, I feel that you have abandoned me."

Everything stopped abruptly. It was quiet.

After a pause the speaker said, "We used to hold sweet converse together; within the silence we walked in harmony and peace. Let my prayer be heard, O comforter. Listen to me, and answer me; I cry out to you in the midst of my pain and distraction!"

Get the picture? We live in a world of incessant distractions, a fast-paced cyber world of cell phones, internet shopping, e-mail, and palm pilots that constantly drags us away from God and our commitment to God's ways. A glut of brilliant images cascades out of our computer screens at ever increasing speed. Sunday morning is a constant balancing act between kids' sports and church. The idea of "quiet time" for prayer and Bible study is totally foreign to a world in which there is constant noise from TVs, stereos, and even the passing traffic. The quiet rhythms of God's Word and God's ways are drowned out by the loud and often strident shouts of our culture.

Out of Synch with God's Rhythm

Many of us know we are out of synch with God's ways and feel that our lives have lost the music God's rhythms should provide. Unfortunately we don't know how to sift through or turn off the noise that surrounds us every day to connect with God. Even though we have more tools than ever before to steer our spiritual journeys, we feel less able to drive toward God and God's ways. Type "Christian" into any internet search engine, and you will get millions of responses. There are hundreds of versions of the Bible available for us to read, endless internet prayer groups to join, and an untold number of Christian audiotapes to play; yet the average time we spend in prayer and Bible study has dropped precipitously in the last ten years. We are even confused about what kind of help we really need and where to look for it.[1]

Tragically this disconnect from spiritual rhythms has had dire consequences for every other area of our lives. Anxiety, depression, loneliness, and suicide are all on the increase. There is growing evidence that stress and the pressures of overbooked schedules contribute to these emotional problems. Even our susceptibility to physical diseases such as high blood pressure, arthritis, and the common cold appears to be affected by our spiritual well-being. As E. Stanley Jones, missionary, author, and Christian statesman of the early twentieth century said almost a hundred years ago, "When I am against the Christian way, I know exactly what happens; I am out of gear; something has slipped a cog, I feel orphaned, estranged, not at home with myself or people or God; my life sags and loses its music; everything within me says: 'This is the unnatural way to live.'"[2]

Have You Lost Your Peace?

Several years ago while working as a medical doctor in Africa, I visited a highly successful health clinic in rural Zaire. This clinic provided more resources for mothers with young children than any other clinic in the country. Mothers and infants attended regularly for shots and well-baby checkups. In spite of this care, many infants died of malnutrition.

"Why didn't you bring your child to see us?" the frustrated nurse asked one mother whose child had just died.

The mother looked puzzled. "But she wasn't sick. She had lost her peace. Western medicine cannot cure misery. I took her to the traditional healer but he couldn't help either."

The clinic nurse suddenly realized she had a serious problem. Her understanding of health and the mother's understanding of health were two totally different things. The nurse knew she would never be able to prevent children from starving unless she could help their mothers understand what physical health looked like.

How many of us have lost our spiritual peace without realizing that we are ill because we have no idea what spiritual health and wholeness look like from God's perspective? How many of us are unable to identify the roots of our spiritual malaise and don't know how to use the prescriptive resources so abundant at our fingertips to restore our spiritual health? Are we starving to death spiritually because we don't know how to eat spiritual food and connect to the godly rhythms that abound around us? Perhaps, like this young mother in Zaire, we are confused because the resources available to us seem to belong to a foreign culture.

A Prescription for Health

From the time the children of Israel came out of Egypt, God showed concern for their health, but God's prescription for health was always very different from that of the surrounding cultures. At the time of Moses' birth, the *Papyrus Ebers,* written about 1552 B.C., would have provided many of the standard treatments for disease. Drugs included "lizards' blood, swines' teeth, putrid meat, stinking fat, moisture from pigs' ears, milk goose grease, asses' hoofs, animal fats, excreta from animals, including human beings, donkeys, antelopes, dogs, cats and even flies."³ It doesn't sound very inspiring to me, and it didn't impress God either.

Health and wholeness from God's perspective have always depended not primarily on the taking of medicine but on obedience to God's Word and commandments. "If you listen carefully to the voice of the LORD your God and do what is right in his eyes, if you pay attention to his commands and keep all his decrees, I will not bring on you any of the diseases I brought on the Egyptians, for I am the LORD who heals you" (Exod. 15:26). Obedience to God's laws provided a rhythm for life that flowed out of the Jewish religious practices and impacted every other area of life—their economic and political relationships, their health and nutritional standards, and even their festivities and celebrations.

For Jews the road to health began with the recognition that they were meant to live by a new value system, a new life that revolved around their restoration to a right relationship to God. However, it encompassed far more than that. It embraced all aspects of a person's being—mind, body, soul, and spirit. It even required the wholeness and well-being of the community, including God's creation.

The biblical word used to represent this kind of health and wholeness is *shalom,* a word that symbolizes Israel's ideal of living in the presence of God and in accordance with God's laws. In his important book *Living Toward a Vision: Biblical Reflections on Shalom,* Walter Brueggemann identifies *shalom* as the biblical word that best describes this all-embracing vision.⁴ He explains that the original meaning of shalom was far more than the usual English translation "peace." "Wholeness" or "completeness" is a better translation, but even these words are inadequate. Shalom is far more than the absence of conflict or the existence of "inner peace." "Shalom is the substance of the Biblical vision of one community embracing all creation. It refers to all those resources and factors which make communal harmony joyous and effective."[5] It embraces God's desire to restore every part of creation and all aspects of life to the wholeness and harmony of relationship with him that was broken through the disruption of the fall.

This vision of shalom and its incredible promise of wholeness and restoration for all of creation is at the center of God's dream for all humanity and for God's world. Richard Foster says, "This great vision of *shalom* begins and ends our Bible. In the creation story God brought order and harmony out of chaos. In the Apocalypse of John we have the glorious wholeness of a new heaven and a new earth."[6] Mennonite missionary James Metzler adds, "From the disruption of *shalom* in the Garden of Eden to its total renewal in the new Jerusalem, the object of all of God's work is the recovery of shalom in his creation."[7]

The Quest for Wholeness

The premise of *Sacred Rhythms: Finding a Peaceful Pace in a Hectic World* is that today all of us are searching for the wholeness of shalom—that ideal quality of living in the presence of God and in accordance with God's laws. We are trying to find the prescription for a healthy life. Like the Israelites we are looking for far more than treatment of our physical ills. We don't just want a cure for the common cold; we want a cure for our disjointed and out-of-step lives. We want to find places to pause for spiritual renewal in the whirlwind of busyness, times to disconnect from the rapid-fire screen images, and ways to turn off the urban clamor. We too want to find a prescription that brings health to every part of life and connects to a rhythm that permeates all that we are and do.

For us too the discovery of real health and wholeness—shalom health—can only come as we embrace a new value system and new rituals and practices that affirm that value system. Just as health for the ancient Israelites was founded on the following of God's laws and practices, so today our health is dependent on the rhythm that our spiritual practices bring to all of life. As with the Israelites, these spiritual practices don't just encompass our private times alone with God; they should permeate every aspect of our lives.

Practice Makes Perfect

The term *spiritual practice* is often used to describe any routine or activity we perform regularly to deepen our intimacy with God. Such practices provide the routines and rituals that undergird and reinforce the values we believe in and the principles by which we live. Spiritual practices form the framework of our lives. They bring us into joyous relationship with God and enable us to discern God's will. They nurture our personal healing processes and shape the communities in which we live and minister.

As people of Christian faith our spiritual practices have three directions. First, we begin with practices that are directed upward toward God and our need to maintain a healthy relationship with God. Second, we need practices that are directed inward toward our own spiritual transformation and personal journey toward wholeness. Third, we need practices that are focused outward toward our relationships in the greater community and toward the needs of our hurting world. God's purpose is that we might be instruments of healing and wholeness to those around us, and our own wholeness is interrelated to the wholeness of all the rest of God's people and even of God's creation.

Interestingly a growing area of research suggests that people who practice regular spiritual observances such as prayer, meditation, and Bible study are less likely to suffer from high blood pressure, depression, and other illnesses. When they get sick, such people tend to recover more quickly than those who don't pray regularly. Recent clinical research suggests that even remote intercessory prayer may significantly impact the course of an illness in an individual's life.[8]

This book is divided into two sections. In the first part we will identify the physical rhythms God built into our bodies and our world. We will use these as a foundation to examine the spiritual rhythms God intends to govern our lives and discover how cooperating with these can enhance and strengthen every part of our lives and faith.

In the second part of the book we will examine practical ways in which we can connect to these essential patterns. We will explore how to develop spiritual practices that can intertwine through our busy schedules, bringing a sense of rhythm to all we do. We will learn to develop a rhythm of daily prayer, weekly Sabbath, and seasonal observances that flows throughout the year, punctuating our activities with times of celebration and reflection. This rhythm undergirds our lives with times for rest, reflection, and refocusing. It provides opportunities for witness and Christian service in the midst of our busy lives. This rhythm moves us toward God's vision and the shalom wholeness God intends for us.

Listen to the Beat

Each chapter ends with a spiritual checkup—a time to pause to take our pulse. We are encouraged to check out our physical health on a regular basis, and we should check out our spiritual health regularly too.

The quest for health and wholeness is central to the human journey. It is also central to God's desire for us to live in the fullness and wholeness that only his ways can provide. Let's be brave, open our ears and eyes, and listen to the beat of God's shalom rhythm in our lives and the world.

1

RUNNING FOR YOUR LIFE

*M*aika sat on the bed in front of me, her long blond hair framing her pale and anxious face.

I had just finished examining her, and I was puzzled. Her heart rate was rapid and decidedly irregular, her blood pressure was too low, and her blood chemistry was totally out of control. I couldn't find a reason for her body's erratic behavior. Until yesterday she had been healthy. Since she was just twenty-five, I couldn't believe she had suddenly developed a heart problem without any obvious cause.

While we waited for the last of her test results, Maika, who was famished after twelve hours of fasting, decided to have a snack. She reached into her purse and pulled out an enormous bag of licorice, which she started to munch one piece after another.

"How long have you been eating licorice like that?" I asked.

"For the last month," she said. "I love the stuff, and my mother just sent me a huge supply of my favorite licorice from Holland."

Suddenly I knew exactly what was causing Maika's out-of-synch rhythm. It was the licorice! Can you imagine that? Eaten in the quantities Maika was consuming, licorice can do devastating things to chemical balance and bodily rhythms. A couple of days on a normal diet without licorice completely restored a healthy rhythm to her heart and her body.

A Time for Everything

Rhythm is an essential part of life and of every aspect of the world around us. The origins of these rhythms are rooted deep within the creation story. God's first act was to create a rhythm of light and darkness. "God called the light 'day' and the darkness he called 'night.' And there was evening, and there was morning—the first day" (Gen. 1:5). This rhythm formed the basis for all of God's continuing acts of creation. As Ecclesiastes reminds us, "There is a time for everything, and a season for every activity under heaven" (Eccles. 3:1). Our God is a God of seasons—a God of rhythm. Just as our heartbeats underlie the rhythms of our bodies, so God's heartbeat—God's rhythm—is meant to underlie the pattern of all activities in our world.

God's creation itself is a wonderful model for the rhythms of God. The sun rises each morning, and light breaks out from the darkness to beckon forth the day. It races across the sky. At a predictable time each evening, its light once more dissolves into the darkness of night. The tides ebb and flow with the phases of the moon. The changing seasons pulse to a rhythm that is ordained by the movement of the earth around the sun. We expect that at a certain time each year spring will burst forth, filled with the glory of God and the promise of new life. We expect the hot balmy days of summer to follow. They nourish the succulent fruit, vegetables, and grains for the autumn harvest. At year's end, we rely on the quiescent but necessary cold gray days of winter to invade our world, providing rest for the soil.

In recent years scientists have discovered that what were once thought to be random and unfathomable changes such as weather fluctuations and disease cycles all have cyclical patterns to them. There is rhythm and order in such mundane and seemingly erratic events as the formation of clouds, the eddying of water in a stream, and the rising of a column of smoke. These incredible God-designed rhythms create some of the most beautiful and intricate patterns imaginable.[1]

The Rhythm of Our Bodies

Our bodies also beat to a rhythm—in fact they beat to a myriad of interconnected rhythms. The one we are most familiar with is the rhythm of the heart. I am amazed that such a deceptively simple muscle can pump blood throughout the body every moment of every day of a person's life, adapting its pace to a person's emotions and changes in activity.

The heart's healthy functioning depends on a very simple rhythm. The cycle begins with a brief period of relaxation during which the heart's chambers fill with blood. Then suddenly an electrical impulse jolts it into action causing the muscle to contract. Blood rushes out of the heart and into the arteries, carrying oxygen and other nutrients to the rest of the body. A second later it happens again and then again and again.

This rhythm is the first sound an infant hears as it lies in its mother's womb. In a normal healthy heart, this rhythm of rest and activity is sustained throughout a person's life. Other rhythms, like hormonal levels, blood pressure, mental alertness, physical strength, and countless other bodily functions ebb and flow in time to an invisible clock, pacing our bodies throughout the day and the seasons of the year.

The most powerful and pervasive rhythms that virtually all living creatures experience are the daily or circadian rhythms—those rhythms that revolve around the continuous cycling of day and night, of sleep and wakefulness. Interestingly organisms cannot cope with too much change to their cycles. If we try to train an organism to a thirty-, thirty-five-, or forty-hour cycle, the creature soon gives up trying to adjust and returns to its original twenty-four-hour cycle.

In human beings there are many biological rhythms that pulse through our bodies in time to this circadian rhythm. When we get up in the morning, hormones and neurotransmitters spring into action, speeding our heart rate, raising our temperature, and adjusting our breathing. Some of these chemical changes tell us when it is time to eat or to exercise. They walk us through our day moment by moment and encourage us to develop a pattern for our physical lives that is in synch with their unconscious promptings. At night a whole new array of hormones are produced to govern our sleeping hours. These encourage us to relax and get ready to go to sleep. They slow our heart rate and breathing, quiet our mental activity, and relax our bodies. Amazingly these rhythms repeat themselves every day, adjusting to the seasons of the year and the changing lengths of day and night.

Even the routines of our days tend to flow to a rhythm. We get up in the morning, jump in the shower, down a quick cup of coffee, and head out the door. Most of us even carry date books or palm pilots to keep track of our schedules and ensure that our rhythms and routines are maintained. Often we feel stressed or irritated if something happens to disrupt the rhythm we are used to.

One interesting aspect of God's rhythms is that though they may follow the same pattern day in and day out, within that structure is room for infinite variety and creativity. If this weren't true, we would never be able to adjust to change at all. Jet lag wouldn't just bother me for a few days, but for the rest of my life. God's rhythms provide both stability and flexibility to life. They are never boringly predictable, yet we can always rely on them. They provide the framework for all that happens in our world. The problem is that our own routines and rhythms are increasingly disconnected from the rhythms and patterns of God's world.

The Disconnected Rhythm

I am a hot weather person. My body functions best when the outside temperature is between 80 and 90 degrees Fahrenheit. In the winter I walk around like the proverbial bag lady clad in multiple layers of clothing. You can imagine my delight a couple of years ago when I received an invitation to go to Florida during the cold rainy days of March. For days beforehand I avidly watched the weather forecast, delighted that the temperatures were a good 20 degrees warmer than in Seattle.

I packed all my summer clothes and headed off—and almost froze to death. The air-conditioned hotel where I stayed would have suited a family of penguins. Once again I waddled around in multiple layers of clothing. For all I knew the outside temperature was below freezing.

Have you noticed how many aspects of our modern culture seem determined to defeat nature's rhythms? Strawberries in winter, apples in summer, air conditioning, central heat-ing, and artificial lighting all make it possible for us to ignore God's patterns of night and day, summer and winter. Our lives are increasingly not only disconnected from the rhythms of God's created world but also in competition with them. At dusk I turn on the lights and extend the day for as long as I like. When it gets cold, I ratchet up the heat, and in the summer I turn on the air conditioning.

Sadly when we embrace unquestioningly these modern innovations, we often miss the beautiful rhythms God has woven into creation and the implications that these patterns have for us. The waxing and waning of the moon with its silvery light shining in the night sky and the lapping of waves against the seashore no longer remind us of the soothing rhythms of God beating through our lives. The slow dawning of each new day with the softly changing colors of the sun rising over the mountains and the awakening of the world in springtime as the daffodils raise their bright yellow heads above the earth no longer bring the promise of hope and resurrection. The comforting darkness of night and the dormancy of winter no longer prompt us to rest. The biological rhythms created by God have been blurred by a world that tells us there is never time to slow down and take a break. Most disturbing of all, our spiritual heartbeats are dangerously offbeat. They have been severely disrupted, and we haven't even noticed.

Do You Need a Pacemaker?

Life without rhythm has dire consequences, as I learned clearly my first night on duty in the emergency room of Christchurch Public Hospital in New Zealand. Not long after I started work, Janet Thompson, a vivacious brunette in her mid-forties, was admitted complaining of fainting attacks.

She was concerned but didn't really think her problem was serious.

At first I was inclined to agree. Janet appeared to be a normal, healthy woman who exercised regularly and ate a healthy diet. Her pulse and blood pressure were normal. Even an electrocardiogram looked healthy. We were about to reassure her and send her home when suddenly she became cold and clammy. She turned deathly pale and collapsed in front of our eyes. As she did so, that seemingly healthy-looking heart rhythm underwent a drastic change. It became rapid and erratic.

Janet was suffering from a cardiac arrhythmia. When her heart beat erratically, the chambers couldn't fill properly and the blood flow was insufficient to provide oxygen to her brain, so she became unconscious. She needed a pacemaker to stimulate her heart and regulate her rhythm, otherwise she would die.

Disruption to our daily and yearly rhythms is just as devastating, as anyone who has suffered from jet lag knows well. Although I love to travel, it doesn't always treat me kindly. No matter where I am in the world, my body clock feels out of control. I am ravenous at midnight and fall asleep in the middle of the day. Even the sudden change from long summer days to long winter darkness that attends north to south travel is disorienting. On one occasion I arrived in Norway on midsummer's eve. Friends knocked on my door at eleven o'clock at night to go sightseeing. We sat on the beach at midnight, eating by the pale glow of the midnight sun. Then I flew to New Zealand where winter was in full swing. I felt as though I had landed on another planet—a land of eternal cold and darkness. We went to work in the dark and came home in the dark, huddling around the fire in the evenings to keep warm. It took me weeks to recover.

Even the seasonal rhythms of our world can be devastated by disruptions to weather patterns that result in floods, droughts, poor harvests, and famines. In *The Little Ice Age,* Brian Fagan documents how the sudden climatic changes of the early fourteenth century from warm and dry to cold and wet contributed to the famines and political and religious turmoil of the time. He believes it led to the spread of the bubonic plague, which killed one-third of the European population. It even laid the foundations for the settlement of North America.[2]

A growing area of medical research is the investigation of the relationship between the physical rhythms of our bodies and our health, and not surprisingly an increasing number of treatments are emerging that link the two. The use of light therapy for conditions like seasonal affective disorder and jet lag is one treatment that has caught attention in recent years. I was relieved when I discovered that I could decrease my jet lag considerably by paying careful attention to the rhythms of day and night at my destination. If I go to bed at the same time each evening, eat meals at regular intervals, and make sure that I spend plenty of time out in the sunlight, then I adjust more quickly. Business travelers who sit for long hours in meetings are discovering that taping small lights behind their knees to simulate daylight relieves their jet lag considerably. No kidding! These lights are the latest fashion accessory for busy travelers!

All of us are aware that a healthy heart and regular daily and yearly rhythms are essential for health. We also know that if our heartbeat is irregular then we need to see a physician for a checkup. Most of us, however, are unaware of the spiritual rhythms that are just as crucial to our health and well-being. Since our lives are increasingly disconnected from the rhythms of God's world, we do not hear the underlying whisper of God's heartbeat that is meant to sustain us and we are unaware of the symptoms that should alert us to our growing ill health. We suffer from spiritual heart problems that are just as life threatening as my patient's physical ailment. We live in a constant state of spiritual arrhythmia but are totally unaware of the severity of our condition or of our need for a spiritual pacemaker to stimulate our lives and regulate our pulse.

Diagnosing Your Spiritual Arrhythmia

Cardiac arrhythmias come in many forms. Some are fairly innocuous—like Maika's licorice problem. Others, like Janet's, can be deadly and require major surgery or a pacemaker to rectify them. In some arrhythmias, the heart beats so rapidly that its chambers can't fill adequately. In other arrhythmias, the heart beats too slowly and the body starves for oxygen. Often the most dangerous arrhythmias cause erratic beats that can be hard to diagnose. The heart misses a beat here and there or speeds up uncontrollably for a brief period and then returns to a normal pattern for a while. Like Janet people with these arrhythmias live with a false sense of security.

Spiritual arrhythmias also come in many forms with a wide range of symptoms. Loneliness, depression, anxiety, stress, low back pain, headaches, and chronic discontent can all have their roots in our spiritual malaise. Even our constant craving to buy and accumulate more stuff can come from a spiritual void within our hearts. "People don't need electronic equipment; they need something worthwhile to do with their lives. People need identity, community, challenge, acknowledgement, love and joy," says Donella Meadows in *Beyond the Limits.* "To try to fill these needs with material things is to set up an unquenchable appetite for false solutions to real and never-satisfied problems. The resulting psychological emptiness is one of the major forces behind the desire for material growth."[3]

Does Normal Compete with God?

Unfortunately the world around us provides many rhythms that compete with God's rhythms—and we are convinced that these abnormal rhythms are normal. "Normal is getting dressed in clothes that you buy for work, driving through traffic in a car you are still paying for, in order to get to the job that you need so you can pay for the clothes, car and the house that you leave empty all day in order to afford to live in it."[4]

For some of us normal is a frenetic lifestyle in which we try to practice our spirituality with the same exhausting rhythm. For others normal has no spiritual pulse at all. Our busyness has crowded out all religious observances and our spiritual heartbeat is getting slower and slower and slower. For still others of us erratic and random is the order of the day. There is no pattern to our spiritual rhythm—we stop and start, pray furiously for a few days and then get distracted by the cares and worries of this world and ignore God all together, hoping that the occasional and irregular prayers we offer will be sufficient to sustain us through the trials of life. In all cases we suffer serious maladies that sap the very life from us.

Arrhythmia #1—The Fast-Paced Digital Beat

Our modern world throbs to a round-the-clock, fast-paced digital beat that is increasingly disconnected from God's rhythms of life. My friend Marie's life is a good example of this. She stumbles out of bed when her alarm rings at 6 A.M., dashes into the shower, downs a quick cup of coffee, and heads for the car to begin her hour-long commute into Seattle. As she drives Marie listens to the early morning news and the stock market report. Then she grabs her cell phone and makes a few quick phone calls to New York in preparation for her day as a stockbroker. If she has time, Marie listens to a Christian worship tape and says a quick prayer during the last few minutes of her trip. This experience has become the mainstay of her spiritual life as her busy schedule allows her little other time for prayer or Bible study.

Marie is committed to her church and her faith and feels that her religious life should be lived at the same frenetic pace as everything else. She normally dashes into church ten minutes late because her son's baseball games are often scheduled for Sunday morning. Sunday afternoons she juggles church missions committee meetings and trips to the mall or supermarket as she endeavors to balance the demands of her family and church with the growing pressure from her work. Like my cardiac patient, Marie knows there is something wrong with her life, but she doesn't think it is serious. She believes that God wants her busy all the time. "If you can't walk with the footmen, how can you expect to run with the horses?" she asked me. The solution to her problem, she believes, is to ratchet up the pace of her life to free up a few more minutes each day for prayer and Bible study.

According to Bart Sparagon of the Meyer Friedman Institute in San Francisco, many of us, like Marie, are suffering from "time urgency." We struggle against time and spend much of our day seeking to control it. Tragically anything that slows us down becomes an obstacle in our way, an enemy that needs to be overcome.[5]

The quest for speed and efficiency dominates our modern lives, and everyone convinces us that this frenetic rhythm is the only one we can adopt—for every area of our lives. Surprisingly, though we all complain about how busy we are and how overloaded our lives have become, speed is still generally viewed as positive, and the people we look up to tend to be the ones who have most bought into this fast-paced, cyber-spaced rhythm. Nothing illustrates this better than the fast-paced TV ads that constantly speed through our lives. Vacuum cleaners, laundry detergents, painkillers, and the latest food fads all appeal more when portrayed with high-speed power and ultra efficiency. They lure us with the promise of whirlwind performance and miraculously speedy efficiency. We are saving time, they all tell us, but time for what? Time to cram more stressed-out living into our overbooked schedules?

"Revving up, in fact, is often heralded as the answer to the problems caused by our overly busy lives," explains Jay Walljasper. "Swamped by the accelerating pace of work? Get a computer that's faster. Feel like your life is spinning out of control? Increase your efficiency by learning to read and write faster. No time to enjoy life? Purchase one of those handy products advertised on television that promise to help you cook faster, exercise faster and even make money faster."[6]

Tragically many of us think that this same kind of rhythm should apply to our spiritual lives. We gulp down a quick prayer in the mornings, listen to a few spiritual songs or an inspirational speaker while we speed to work, and race into church on Sunday for a quick fix before zooming to the mall to catch up on the week's shopping. Unfortunately our faith communities often seem to applaud rather than question this way of life. As the ad for a local Christian bookstore web site suggested, "Can't sleep—may as well go shopping." No wonder the relentless pace of our lives masks a very rapid spiritual arrhythmia that never seems able to pump quite enough spiritual life into our bodies. In our busyness we miss the whispering voice through which God often speaks and the life-giving rhythm that God intends to sustain us.

Elijah—God's Offbeat Prophet

The inability to juggle the demands of a busy life with the spiritual rhythms God intends is not a new problem. Even some of

God's most dedicated followers have crashed and burned because they allowed their lives to get out of synch with God's rhythms. Take Elijah in 1 Kings 19, for example. Here is an out-of-synch individual if ever I saw one. Have you ever thought about why this wonderful man of God, who had just shown the miraculous power of God to thousands of people, would suddenly flee from a single woman (Jezebel) and go to hide in the desert?

As I read this story, I get the impression that like so many of us, Elijah was just too busy to take time for God. In the hectic whirl of activity, Elijah had disconnected from the spiritual rhythm he needed to sustain him. Without that life-sustaining pulse, he didn't just run away; he wanted to die—not exactly the reaction we would expect from a great prophet of God. Surprisingly God doesn't admonish Elijah for not working harder or rap him over the knuckles because he can't cope with the pressure. Nor does God chastise him for his lack of spiritual endurance. God sees Elijah's exhaustion and reaches out to offer him what all of us need when we disconnect from God and lose our rhythm—rest, food, and refreshment. Then and only then does God take him to Horeb, the mountain of God, a place where Elijah can have a fresh personal encounter with the living God.

The scary thing is that in his stressed-out state Elijah seems to have lost his ability to hear God's voice—that caressing whisper that gently seeks to direct and guide us. Unfortunately many of us suffer from the same problem. Our spiritual arrhythmias have so disconnected us from God and his whispering voice that we no longer hear what God is saying and we are incapable of reestablishing God's beat in our hearts.

Arrhythmia #2—The Plugged-In Cyber Beat

Bob, a busy employee of one of the Seattle dot.coms, has chosen a different solution for his life. He regularly works a seventy-hour week, often starting at 5 A.M. so that he has time in the evenings to rush home to be with his wife and kids. When he is home, Bob spends a growing amount of time on-line, keeping in touch by e-mail, banking, and participating in chat room conversations. Bob has even found an internet church that provides a feeling of spiritual community. He stopped going to a real church several months ago because it seemed like one more pressure in his already overworked schedule. Sunday morning is the only time he can relax. A good football game is far more satisfying to him than any church service. Bob sees his job as God's blessing and therefore feels that he needs to accept all the time pressures and responsibilities that come with it.

The growing pressure we all face to be plugged into our work 24/7 reinforces the idea that the pace and rhythm of every day is meant to be the same as that of every other day. So-called timesaving innovations crank up the pace of life to unimaginable levels, blurring our impressions of time and space, of work and rest. Jet travel zips us across continents in a few hours. Cell phones, fax machines, and e-mail instantly link us to friends and colleagues half a world away any time of the day or night. The advent of twenty-four-hour e-commerce, drive-through windows, and ATM machines all convince us that there is no need to rest or slow down.

Even when we take a day off or go on vacation we feel we can no longer disconnect. A recent *Newsweek* poll showed that 34 percent of travelers checked their voice mail or answering machine at least once during their vacations and 14 percent checked it daily. The article showed a young man perched on top of a 12,000-foot mountain with his laptop open, getting his e-mail. "The solution, increasingly is to remain plugged in: by fax, e-mail, mobile phone, pager. These devices are the furniture of what is becoming, for many travelers, the global *workspace,* forever blurring the boundaries between office and vacation."[7] The blurring of such boundaries drowns out all other rhythms and provides little space for spiritual life.

In his book *Bowling Alone: The Collapse and Revival of American Community,* Robert Putnam documents the precipitous decline of American involvement in all kinds of religious activities. Though people may still call themselves Christians and may even attend formal church services on Sunday morning, their involvement in all other church-related activities is far less than it was in the 1960s. "In sum, over the last three to four decades Americans have become 10 percent less likely to claim church membership, while our actual attendance and involvement in religious activities has fallen by roughly 25 to 50 percent."[8]

The blurring of boundaries between work and vacation means that church-related activities often have little if any relevance to the pace or rhythm of life. Bob and people like him are suffering from serious spiritual blockage. Their spiritual heartbeat is slowing to the crisis point where sudden spiritual death is likely to occur.

Arrhythmia #3—The Stop-and-Start Beat

Paula is a twenty-year-old student at Wheaton College. She attends chapel twice a week and regularly attends dorm prayer meeting during term time, but when she goes home to Southern California her spiritual life takes a dive. During break she hangs out at the local mall with her friends and has little time left for prayer and Bible study. She rarely lets a day go by without purchasing some item of clothing. She lives for the sales and the bargains she can buy to take back to college to impress her fellow students.

Our modern consumer culture exerts growing pressure on us to buy more and to increasingly derive our meaning and sense of purpose from the clothes we wear and the cars we drive. In *Enchanting a Disenchanted World,* George Ritzer contends that the consumer culture deliberately draws us into a new religion, a "religion of consumption." In so doing, it gathers us into its new places for worship—the shopping malls. "Malls provide the kind of centeredness traditionally provided by religious temples, and they are constructed to have similar balance, symmetry, and order. Their atriums usually offer connection to nature through water and vegetation. People gain a sense of community as well as more specific community services. Play is almost universally part of religious practice, and malls provide a place for people to frolic. Similarly malls offer a setting in which people can partake in ceremonial meals. Malls clearly qualify for the label of cathedrals of consumption."[9]

Unfortunately even our faith has become commercialized, often in superficial and sometimes embarrassing ways. "Spread the Word!" burbles the text on the back of a pack of air fresheners emblazoned with a portrait of Jesus walking barefoot through a flock of sheep. Jesus now saves from the embarrassment of unpleasant and antisocial smells. "Express your feelings with this beautiful, meaningful air freshener. Use it anywhere . . . wherever a pleasant aroma is desired or an odor problem exists."[10] If that is a little too hard to accept, how about Heaven's Best chocolate bar? "Now you can truly devour the Word! Simply break open a Heaven's Best chocolate bar, each one 'gracefully carved in the shape of four open Bibles,' and discover for yourself that the scriptures are 'sweeter than honey to my mouth' . . . taste and see that the Lord is good."[11] It is not surprising that our visits to the mall set the rhythm and pattern of our lives rather than our involvement in church.

For many, religion has become just another commodity to consume rather than a renewed way of life. "People are looking at churches in a similar cost-benefit analysis they'd give to any other consumer purchase," said David Kinnaman from Barna Research in a recent article in the *New York Times.* "There is little brand loyalty. Many are looking for the newest and the greatest."[12] Unfortunately a growing number of churches cater to this market. They provide a "full-service 24/7 sprawling village, which offers many of the conveniences and trappings of secular life wrapped around a spiritual core. It is possible to eat, shop, go to school, bank, work out, scale a rock-climbing wall and pray there, all without leaving the grounds."[13]

The problem with this kind of environment, and the rhythm of life it propounds, is that it sanctions rather than questions the prevailing culture. It encourages us to withdraw and insulate ourselves from the world rather than to engage in it and witness to God's love and compassion. Tragically when we withdraw from the hurting world around us, we also withdraw from God. Although our spiritual life may seem vibrant on the surface, underneath it is little more than a faint flutter. The values that govern our lives and the events that shape them have little to do with our religious beliefs and give evidence of an unhealthy spiritual arrhythmia.

Crashing in the Fast Lane

Several years ago I experienced my own disconnected and out-of-synch rhythm. Like Elijah, I was so busy being zealous for God that I did not take the time to renew and replenish my spiritual life. I ended up in the hospital—on my forty-first birthday! I remember lying perfectly still, my chalk-white hand feebly clasping the hospital blankets. My breath came in short agonizing gasps, and my chest was constricted with pain. I felt my whole system was shutting down as I gently faded out of the world. For the next two days a cardiac monitor recorded my every beat as the doctors puzzled over my problem. Had I suffered a heart attack? Was my heart rhythm out of synch?

"Can you think of what the problem might be?" my doctor asked.

As a physician I should be able to diagnose my own complaint, shouldn't I? Even my brain had shut down, and I couldn't string two logical thoughts together let alone think about what was going on in my body.

Over the next few months during my protracted convalescence, I spent time reflecting on what had brought me to that place and how I could have avoided it. The underlying cause was a viral illness, but I am convinced that my body rebelled against my fast-paced, high-stress lifestyle. I had abused my body. I had lived in a state of constant spiritual arrhythmia and had left too little time and energy to recharge my "battery." Now I was paying the price.

Listen to the Beat—Are You Suffering from Spiritual Arrhythmia?

How can we tell if we are suffering from a serious spiritual arrhythmia? How do we diagnose our problem early enough to avoid the consequences?

If you are really hooked into cyberspace you may like to wait and try some of the methods suggested by an article I read on a recent plane flight. This article suggested that in the future computer chips would be imbedded in everything from lightbulbs to bicycles. "Your tiny wireless heart monitor will connect with your blood pressure analyzer, your wireless weigh scale will talk to your PDA or cell phone, and all of these gadgets will consult your doctor via the Internet. Your refrigerator, oven, microwave and toaster may even supply data about your food input."[14] In the future you won't need annual checkups and doctor's visits to tell if your heart is missing beats. When something goes wrong with your heart, you will be able to have "an ongoing digitally enabled dialogue" with your health care providers.

In the absence of such sophisticated technology, however, you might like to start where I would start when a person is concerned about his or her heart—by checking your pulse.

Do you feel your life is out of synch with God's intended rhythm? Do you find you are always too busy for prayer and Bible study? Are you running on empty and not sure what to do about it? If so, find a quiet place where you can draw aside and check your pulse. Get out a notebook and get to work.

1. *Are you satisfied with where you are in your Christian journey? Write a short paragraph that honestly expresses how you feel about your present spiritual condition.*
2. *What do you do now on a regular basis to nurture your spiritual growth? Make a list of the activities you perform on a daily, weekly, and yearly basis that provide for your spiritual growth.*
3. *What sets the rhythm for your life? List the major activities you perform on a daily, weekly, and yearly basis that shape the rhythm of your life.*

2

Do You Hear the Beat?

I love hiking and several years ago had a wonderful opportunity to trek through the mountains in Colorado in midsummer. It was a breathtaking experience. Craggy snow-covered peaks rose in majestic splendor in sharp contrast to the lush green valleys through which we walked. A field of wildflowers carpeted the valley floor with splashes of red and gold and purple and blue. Elk and deer dotted the distant hills, and birds sang joyously in the crisp mountain air. We crunched along the pathway in our heavy walking boots in harmony with the beauty of God's creation.

Then we hit the mountain pass. As we climbed above 10,000 feet that beautiful rhythm I had established faltered. My breathing came in short agonizing gasps as I gulped for air in the thin mountain atmosphere. My heart raced, and I puffed and panted up the incline one painful step at a time. Then I stopped, pretending I was admiring the wonderful array of wildflowers that carpeted the surrounding hills. I waited until my heart stopped pounding, caught my breath, and headed off again—but this time at a slower, more measured pace. Reestablishing my rhythm was a conscious effort that required both discipline and practice. Fortunately I had some help from one of my companions who was an expert hiker and who was not deceived by my sightseeing stops. Doug knew I was faking it! After he reached the top, he came back, shouldered my pack, and headed off again at an effortless pace.

Even without my pack I struggled. My body just wasn't fit enough to cope with the added effort I expected of it. But as I consciously breathed in and out in synch with my footsteps and deliberately walked to a measured rhythm, something remarkable happened. My heart rate slowed, my breathing improved, and amazingly my walking pace increased.

In Synch with God's Rhythm

Finding our rhythm in a world that constantly leaves us gasping for breath isn't easy. What kind of a rhythm is best for our lives? Most of us can't or don't want to totally disconnect from the high-speed world in which we live. On the other hand, we don't want to settle for that agonizing rhythm that leaves us gasping for air when life gets tough. What most of us are looking for is a rhythm that both paces us through the everyday and sustains us through the mountain passes—a life with a measured beat and a sense of balance between work and rest, job responsibilities and personal commitments.

In the secular world there is a growing recognition of the need for this kind of balance. In recent years helping employees to balance work and personal commitments has become a priority for many managers. There is a rapidly increasing demand for "life coaches" to help people embrace a new rhythm for their lives. According to Suzette Corr, director of VicHealth's business development and workplace program, companies increasingly are keen to be seen as good employers with family-friendly policies and an interest in creating healthy workplaces. She says that in today's stressful world, workers need a sense of control over their work and personal lives and support for their physical and psychological health if they are to remain motivated and productive.[1]

Even our obsession with fast food is being questioned by a growing number of people around the world. Started in Rome in 1986 as a direct response to the opening of a McDonald's restaurant in the famous Piazza di Spagna, the Slow Food movement is gaining momentum. Dedicated to preserving and supporting traditional ways of growing, producing, and preparing food, the movement's manifesto declares that "a firm defense of quiet material pleasure is the only way to oppose the universal folly of Fast Life."[2] The organization has sixty-five thousand members in forty-five countries and is a growing movement in the United States. "In today's consumer culture, Slow Food may have a message particularly attuned to the culture of the day: a kind of pleasure-loving environmentalism that does not reject consumption per se, but rather the homogenization and high-speed frenzy of chain-store, fast-food life."[3] The Italian leaders feel that rather than being afraid of McDonald's they can take it on and win.

Christians everywhere are also looking for a new beat and crave a rhythm that brings balance to their lives. They too want to take on the frenzied pace of the McDonald's world and win. They are crying out for life coaches, mentors, and spiritual directors to help. At the center of this balanced rhythm for people of faith, however, is the recognition that there is another dimension to life that the secular world does not offer—the rhythm of prayer, Bible study, and spiritual observances that should regulate everything. This kind of rhythm makes time for all the good things that God calls us to be a part of not only for prayer, Bible study, and Christian service but also for the creative activity of work, the joy of relationships, and the soothing relaxation of rest. This is the life that beats in synch with the God-created rhythms within our world—what I like to think of as the heartbeat of God.

The Heartbeat of God

From the beginning of time, the spiritual life of individuals and their communities provided the rhythms and patterns that governed all other daily activities. For the Jews in particular this spiritual rhythm, which emanated from a personal relationship with a loving and caring God, was of paramount importance. "The philosopher Abraham Joshua Heschel spoke of 'holiness in time' as a basic characteristic of Jewish religious practice. Prayer in the morning, afternoon and evening punctuates time in every day. Each week the Sabbath sanctifies time in an evening and day set apart from all others. Jews greet every new month as sacred time, celebrated through prayer and ceremony. And throughout the year a continuous cycle of holidays and festivals gives a sense of spiritual renewal to the passing time."[4]

One of my favorite Old Testament characters who obviously took this kind of spiritual commitment very seriously is Daniel. As a young man he was taken as a slave to the equivalent of the big bad city—Babylon. He was supposed to be fully integrated into the life and ways of the Babylonian people.

Daniel refused to give up the ways of his faith, believing that following God is even more important than life itself.

First, he refused to eat the royal food and drink the royal wine (Dan. 1:8). Amazingly he was found to be healthier than all the other young men. Then he refused to give up his faith observances, in spite of a royal decree that outlawed such practices. "Three times a day he got down on his knees and prayed, giving thanks to his God, just as he had done before" (Dan. 6:10). Of course the story ends with God rescuing Daniel from the lions' den.

Many of us can identify with the dilemmas that Daniel faced in Babylon. Being willing to live by a different set of rules and to a different rhythm than that of the world around us is not easy. Like Daniel we can feel we are throwing ourselves into the lions' den. We are confronted incessantly by the diets of the world and tempted to eat the "royal food." Yet taking the radical step to refuse this diet or being willing to say no when asked to do something that will strip us of our faith observances may have some hidden benefits for our physical and emotional health and even for our workplace productivity. Perhaps it can be a witness to others around us too.

The Rhythm of Health and Wholeness

The heart depends on a rhythm of rest and work to keep it healthy, and so does our spiritual life. Prayer and Bible study, fasting and feasting, Sabbath rest and work are meant to beat through our lives, pacing our days and the cycles of our months and years. Just as our physical hearts send life-giving blood pulsing through our bodies, so these spiritual rhythms are intended to send life-giving nourishment throughout our spiritual bodies. And just as our physical pulse adapts itself to the speeding up and slowing down of life, so our spiritual pulse is meant to respond to life's ups and downs.

Surprisingly a physically fit person usually has a slower heart rate than those who lead sedentary lives. When athletes run or climb a 12,000-foot mountain, their pulse does not increase as rapidly as yours or mine might, and they certainly don't need to stop for "sightseeing breaks" like I did. Each beat of their heart is far more effective in the way it pumps blood throughout their body.

A well-developed spiritual rhythm does the same. It doesn't speed up the pace of life but rather slows it down to a fit and healthy rhythm. Unlike an unhealthy rhythm that fluctuates wildly with our changing activities, a healthy rhythm is consistent and stable, but with an inbuilt flexibility that allows it to respond in a measured way to the ups and downs of our lives. Amazingly this kind of rhythm makes us more effective and more productive.

Of course establishing such a rhythm isn't something that happens by chance—and we can't fake it either. Just as it took me time, effort, and discipline to establish a rhythm that would enable me to climb that mountain pass in Colorado, so it takes time, effort, and discipline to establish our spiritual rhythms and to develop a way of life that flows out of a spiritual center. As I discovered, the best way to establish that rhythm is to stop, catch your breath, and then consult those expert life coaches that God has provided to direct our paths.

The Jesus Rhythm—The Only Way to Live

How do we find God's rhythm and allow it to breathe life into every aspect of our daily routines? How do we balance the busyness of work and family responsibilities with the refreshment of prayer and Sabbath rest without overwhelming ourselves with another series of time commitments? How do we discover what that rhythm is meant to look like?

When I studied cardiology, I spent a lot of time looking at normal heart rhythms before I learned about abnormal ones. Similarly if we want to understand the rhythm that should be at the center of our lives, we need to know what a healthy rhythm looks like. There is no better place to find that rhythm than by looking at the greatest "life coach" of all time—Jesus, the one that E. Stanley Jones calls the "revealer of the nature of life."[5] Jones says that life "works in His way and only in His way."

This way, the way of Christ, is written into the very makeup of our being—into our blood, our nerves, our tissues, and our relationships.[6] We are made to live in intimate relationship with God and to focus outwardly in compassionate care and mutual concern for others. Our bodies, emotions, and spirits function best when we are in step with God and his purposes. The root of all our discontent and striving, the reason for our out-of-synch rhythms, and even the cause of much of our physical illness is "homesickness for God."[7] The only place we will ever find real enjoyment and satisfaction is when we return home to follow the path that God through Christ marks out for us.

Jones explains that in Jesus "God is speaking to us in the only language we can understand, a human language; showing us his life in the only way we could grasp it, a human life; uncovering his character in the place where your character and mine are wrought out, a human character, Jesus is the human life of God."[8] If Jesus was serious about offering us abundant life and if he is "the way, the truth, and the life" (John 14:6 KJV), then the rhythms and patterns of his life must provide the best model for how our lives are meant to look.

Let's walk with Jesus through his daily life, examining how he used his time and resources. I guarantee that as we draw close to him we will find ourselves hungering for what

Jesus had—a life of intimacy with the living God, a life that flowed to rhythms as God intended, not to the rhythms of the Roman and Jewish worlds in which he lived. As theologian N. T. Wright explains, "The closer we get to the original Jesus—to the storytelling Jesus, the healing Jesus, the welcoming Jesus, the Jesus who declared God's judgment on those who rejected the way of peace and justice—the closer we come to the kingdom-of-God Jesus, the closer we are to recognizing the face of the living God."[9]

A Walk with Jesus

Can you imagine what it would have been like to walk with Jesus down those dusty roads of Israel hoping to touch the hem of his garment and receive healing? Several years ago on my first visit to Israel, I sat for hours by the Sea of Galilee, imagining I lived during Jesus' time. I mentally walked along the beach by the ruins of Capernaum, picturing Jesus walking toward me surrounded by eager and expectant crowds. Suddenly he stopped and jumped into a fishing boat, telling Peter and John to push it out from the shore so we all could hear. I shaded my eyes to avoid the glare of the sun glinting on the water. I told my neighbors to be quiet because I didn't want to miss a word of what this brilliant speaker had to say. And I needed to listen closely because in those days there were no megaphones or sound systems to amplify his voice.

I imagined following Jesus to Jerusalem at festival time to hear him preach in the synagogue. I walked down the narrow alleyways with boisterous crowds pushing and shoving me from every angle so that I had trouble keeping my balance. I bumped into barrows laden with figs and dates and rich aromatic spices. Then I watched in astonishment as Jesus reached out and touched a woman I knew who was bent and crippled since my childhood. As I watched, Jesus straightened her back. And she came toward me, singing, dancing, and praising God for her healing.

Jesus literally carried the weight of the world on his shoulders. The pressure to heal the sick, feed the hungry, and preach good news to the poor must have been enormous. Yet he rarely hurried and never appeared to be stressed out. There was a rhythm to his life that others craved—a rhythm we could all benefit from.

What are the keys to his extremely productive yet apparently relaxed lifestyle and to his incredible intimacy with God? How did he prioritize his use of time and energy? What lessons can we learn for our lives?

The Importance of Purpose

The first thing that impresses my husband, Tom, and me about Jesus is the *single-minded purpose* with which he lived. In our recent book *Living on Purpose: Finding God's Best for Your Life*, we said, "One cannot read the gospels without being impressed with the whole-life character of Jesus' faith and how single-mindedly he devoted his life to seeing God's kingdom come on earth as it is in heaven."[10] Jesus' life was singularly focused on revealing the character of God and the values and characteristics of God's kingdom to those he met. He repeatedly showed his disciples and followers that God was a loving, compassionate being who heard their cries and cared about their needs. Time after time Jesus led people out of the bondage of old oppressions into new freedoms. He set them free from the fear of hunger by providing food, and even likened the new kingdom to a great banquet. He released the guilt-ridden from the burden of sin with the promise of forgiveness and reconciliation. He came to those who were poor, overlooked, and marginalized with the assurance that in God's eyes they were as valuable as the wealthy and powerful. To all humankind Jesus offered the hope of a new life and a new beginning.

As we read the Gospels, it is obvious that this strong sense of call provided the rhythm for Jesus' life. Because he knew exactly what God had called him to do, he knew precisely how to apportion his time—when to preach, when to heal, and when to walk away from the crowds to disappear for prayer or an intense time of teaching with his disciples. He even knew when to say no to good things he was asked to do that did not reflect God's purposes. He also knew when to make that challenging decision to give up what must have been the most successful healing ministry in the history of our planet to walk toward Jerusalem and the horror of the cross.

The place to start our search for a new rhythm is with a clear sense of God's purpose for our lives. Only when we are as clear as Jesus was about God's kingdom purposes will we have any hope of establishing the kind of rhythm God intends for us. In *Living on Purpose,* Tom and I suggested that the best way to accomplish this is by developing a biblically focused mission statement. We use this to establish goals not just for our vocation but for every area of life—our spiritual life, our community involvement, and even our celebrations.[11] However, knowing we need to set goals that flow out of our faith isn't always enough to keep us from the deceptive allure of the world. We need to follow Jesus in allowing these goals to shape the rhythm of our lives too.

The Rhythms of the Spirit

We don't have to look far before we realize that Jesus' amazing ability to maintain his focus and prioritize his time flowed out of his incredibly intimate relationship to God, the likes of which Jesus' followers had never seen. Like most Jews of his time, Jesus would have prayed several times a day, been well grounded in the Jewish scriptures, and regularly attended the synagogue on the Sabbath day (Luke 4:17). He also celebrated the feasts and festivals of the Jewish religious year.

Unlike the observances of many Jewish leaders, however, Jesus' spiritual life was far more than the ritual recitation of prayers. It was a rich and vital expression of an intimate relationship with God nurtured by hours spent in God's presence. As he walked and talked with God, Jesus listened to God, learned from God, and directed his life according to God's instructions. "I have come . . . to do the will of him who sent me" (John 6:38) was not just a trite saying for Jesus, it was the very essence of all he was and did.

In his classic book on spiritual disciplines, *The Celebration of Discipline*, Richard Foster says, "In prayer, real prayer, we begin to think God's thoughts after Him; to desire the things He desires, to love the things He loves."[12] Through the intimacy of prayer we learn, like Jesus did, to act as God wants us to act. For Jesus, time with God *took priority over* everything else, and it *set the priorities* for everything else. No wonder Jesus withdrew frequently to lonely places to pray, often getting up at unearthly hours of the morning to do so. Sometimes he left crowds of people waiting to be healed (Mark 1:35–39). Or he stayed up all night. Out of those prayer times came a sensitivity to God's Spirit that astounded all who followed him. The disciples hungered for this same kind of relationship. And this God with a human face stunned them by saying that this intimate relationship with God was available to them too.

The rhythm of Jesus' life was a direct result of those protracted times he spent on prayer retreats out in the wilderness or in lonely places. He never made a major decision about where or how to minister or even about which disciples to draw into his inner circle without spending at least *a night* in prayer, listening to God's direction for the days ahead. Before Jesus initiated his ministry, he spent a mammoth forty days in the wilderness, fasting and praying (Matt. 4:1–11). I wonder how many fewer mistakes we would make and how much less stress we would experience if we were willing to make this kind of commitment—well, maybe not forty days in the wilderness but at least a day or two!

A New Approach to Crisis Management

I am fascinated by the way Jesus responded to the desperate crowds that followed him. Having worked as a physician in Africa where we were often thronged by crowds of sick people begging for healing, I know how overwhelming the impact of human suffering can be. Our hearts ached for the children with gross deformities that disfigured their bodies. Sometimes we stretched our operating hours to accommodate another desperate patient. Yet at times Jesus left a lot of sick people behind and walked on to another town. Through prayer he had gained such sensitivity to the Holy Spirit that he could move on, confident that he had accomplished the task God gave him to perform (Mark 1:35–39). Leaving behind people who still needed his healing touch was not something we would expect of a highly successful healer.

Sometimes Jesus' constant prayers led him in unexpected directions. When his friend Lazarus was ill, Jesus didn't race to his aid. Instead, "he stayed where he was two more days" (John 11:6) because he knew "this sickness will not end in death. No, it is for God's glory so that God's Son may be glorified through it" (John 11:4). From my perspective as a medical doctor, that is absolutely the wrong way to respond. After all when someone, particularly a friend, is sick we know it is time to move into high gear with all the life-saving medicine and technology we have available. In any crisis, we always use the most spectacular heroic approach we can muster.

Listening to God isn't easy especially when we are operating in crisis mode, and if we are not in the habit of prayer then it is even more difficult. Hearing God say, "Wait," be it two days, a week, or a month, is almost impossible when we crave activity. What did Jesus do during those two days of seeming inactivity? Perhaps he was praying, asking God, "What do you want me to do in this situation?" The result in the case of Lazarus was a resurrection far more miraculous than another healing would have been.

Even more surprising is that after only three short years Jesus deliberately turned his back on what was the most successful healing ministry in history. "He resolutely set out for Jerusalem" (Luke 9:51) although he knew it would alienate a lot of his followers and ultimately mean his death. Jesus' sensitivity to prayer often led him to do the opposite of what was expected. We expect that if a ministry is successful then God *must* intend it to flourish and grow. Once we start a ministry we rarely check with God about the next steps, yet when we burn out we blame God for our exhaustion. The attraction of worldly success often clouds our vision of God's will. Before we know it we are heading straight back into the stress-filled lifestyle of our world.

The Rhythm of Community

In addition to making time for intimate fellowship with God, the second priority Jesus established was the *importance of community*. He spent more time developing a community of followers than he did preaching. Missiologist Lesslie Newbigin explains it this way: "What did occupy the center of Jesus' concern was the calling and binding to himself of a living community of men and women who would be the witnesses of what he was and did. The new reality that he introduced into history was to be continued through history in the form of a community, not in the form of a book."[13]

It is not surprising therefore that Jesus was usually found in a crowd, often with his twelve disciples, teaching, encouraging, and developing relationships. He modeled a wonderful on-the-job apprenticeship program. At times "Jesus did not want anyone to know where they were, because he was teaching his disciples" (Mark 9:30–31). It is amazing to see how much trust Jesus placed in these disciples and how quickly he delegated major responsibilities to them. He sent them on mission trips and gave them the opportunity to heal and to preach after only a short time of instruction. After only three years of ministry, he literally left them on their own to complete the great task of spreading the gospel throughout the world.

Jesus' disciples were more than just his work companions; they were his closest friends. They obviously experienced a rich sense of community, sharing food and good fellowship, celebrating the Jewish feasts, laughing, and enjoying life together. Wherever Jesus went, he drew others to him in joy and celebration and laughter. In his fascinating book *The Challenge of Jesus,* N. T. Wright tells us, "Wherever Jesus went, there seemed to be a celebration; the tradition of festive meals at which Jesus welcomed all and sundry is one of the most securely established features of almost all recent scholarly portraits."[14]

Even after his resurrection Jesus comes to his followers as a friend and companion. How amazing! Here he has a short forty days in which to establish his follow-up plan. How pressurized can you get! We would expect him to be out preaching, healing, and feeding all he met. Instead, we find him spending time with his friends—encouraging the women who have come to his grave (John 20:11–18), walking quietly with two friends on the road to Emmaus (Luke 24:13–35), and making breakfast for his closest disciples down on the beach in Galilee (John 21:1–14).

Howard Snyder comments, "If Jesus Christ actually gave more time to preparing a community of disciples than to proclaiming the good news (which he did), then the contemporary Church must also recognize the importance of community for proclamation."[15] Making time for friends and family, building up coworkers, and taking time out for fun, fellowship, and celebration were not only important priorities in Jesus' life but also helped set the rhythm of his life. They should do the same for our lives. How wonderful!

The Rhythm of Service

Of course Jesus did spend much of his time working, but it was work with a definite purpose. For Jesus, the goal of work was not necessarily to put bread on the table—that was something for which he encouraged his followers to trust God. For Jesus, work was *focused on service to God and his kingdom purposes.* Work flowed out of the same rhythm that he had established when he set the priority of prayer and time with God.

I can imagine Jesus sitting out in those lonely places and asking God, "What is it that you want me to accomplish today? How can I further the purposes of your kingdom today?"

Since we are representatives of God, Jesus suggests that our work, like his, should be focused on the purposes of God's kingdom. We are meant to bring hope, helping those around us look forward to a world in which there will be no more crying or hunger or pain. In his helpful book on a theology of work, Miroslav Volf comments, "Human work, properly understood theologically, is related to the goal of all history, which will bring God, human beings, and the nonhuman creation into 'shalomic' harmony."[16] One of the basic questions we should constantly be asking God is "What do you want me to accomplish in my work today that will enable me to be a model of your kingdom?"

The Rhythm of Rest

I was relieved when I realized that Jesus believed in work *and in rest.* He recognized that rest was a necessary part of life. He didn't deny the Sabbath; he came to show how it was meant to look. On one occasion "because so many people were coming to be healed that they did not even have a chance to eat, he said to them, 'Come with me by yourselves to a quiet place and get some rest'" (Mark 6:31). He encouraged his followers by saying, "Come to me, all you who are weary and burdened, and I will give you rest" (Matt. 11:28).

The business world is far ahead of the Christian community in recognizing this need. A recent article in *American Demographics* proclaimed, "Taking a break has never seemed so tempting. Driven by a multitude of factors—from layoffs to burnout to the lingering effects of September 11—the idea of taking time out is seducing a significant percentage of Americans. . . . Anecdotal evidence suggests a wide range of Americans are jumping at the chance to get off the reality treadmill temporarily."[17] Evidently a growing number of people are taking time out for a rest. Increasing numbers of students take a "gap" year between high school and college. Others switch jobs frequently and leave time off between. Sometimes burnout is the motivating force, but often people recognize the need to de-stress and renew their focus.

Rest and sleep are essential for health. One small town in Denmark even legislated an hour siesta for its employees recently because of the research that suggested our afternoon productivity is vastly improved by a rest. In Greenwich, Connecticut, one of America's wealthiest communities, the high school has started a Power Nap Club to help students learn to relax and manage their busy lives. Their motto is "Veni vidi dormivi—I came, I saw, I slept."[18] Yet insomnia is an epidemic that is sweeping through our communities. One in four adult Americans suffers from some form of sleeplessness,[19] and we spend millions of dollars each year on sleeping pills, herbal remedies, soothing music, and eye covers to help induce sleep. God, however, invites us to find a rhythm to life that brings a much more renewing rest—a rest for both bodies and spirits.

Disciples Discover a New Rhythm

For Jesus' early disciples too, faith and their spiritual observances provided the central focus for their rhythm of life—the cohesive force binding all else together. They saw themselves as belonging to a new culture, "a third race"—neither Jew nor Gentile but a new and holy nation or people.[20] The values of this kingdom-of-God culture turned a person's life upside down, radically impacting the way Christians viewed their jobs, relationships, and daily activities.

Missiologist David Bosch believes Christians created a new rhythm for life that became the cohesive force in their world. "The way in which they held the world together was, preeminently, through their practice of love and service to all."[21] The early Christian communities were known for the ways they reached out to the poor and marginalized. The evidence shows that these communities grew rapidly because they healed the sick, fed the hungry, and provided a loving, caring community in which all people were welcomed. Just as Jesus' life revolved around a rhythm of spiritual observance, community, work, and rest, so did the lives of the early disciples. "They devoted themselves to the apostles' teaching and to the fellowship, to the breaking of bread and to prayer. Every day they continued to meet together in the temple courts. They broke bread in their homes and ate together with glad and sincere hearts, praising God and enjoying the favor of all the people" (Acts 2:42, 46–47).

The Monastic Rhythm

Jesus and those early disciples are not the only ones who model godly spiritual rhythms for us. Throughout the history of Christianity, sincere followers of Christ have taken seriously the new life and rhythm God intends for us.

Between A.D. 251 and 356 the first monk, St. Antony, abandoned the comfortable life of his time to live in the Egyptian desert. He strove to center his entire life on God alone. He developed a rhythm of prayer, meditation on Scripture, manual work, discipline, and ascetic practices to accomplish this. He was a hermit and a lover of the solitary life in the desert, but he attracted a community of disciples whom he encouraged to remain faithful to the rhythm of the monastic life they had chosen. His wonderful example inspired generations of religious men and women and contributed greatly to the expansion of the monastic movement in early Christian history.[22]

The Celtic Christian monks who established monastic communities throughout Ireland, Britain, and Europe in the fifth through ninth centuries were one group that was influenced by Antony's teaching. They also lived to a rhythmic pace that revolved around spiritual observances, community, and work. Though many of the Celtic monks began life as hermits, they too drew to themselves disciples who craved a holistic spiritual rhythm.

As the monastic centers grew, thriving communities of craftspeople and farmers grew with them. The ringing of bells at regular intervals reminded craftspeople, farmers, and the entire community that their local monastic community was interrupting its work for prayer. It invited them also to interrupt their work and punctuate their own pattern of life with regular times of prayer. People paused where they were in the fields, in their houses, and in their businesses to recite a short service or "office," which they had memorized.

In *The Celtic Way of Prayer*, Esther de Waal says, "Early Celtic Christianity was above all monastic. People learned their religious beliefs and practices from the monastic communities with the monastic ideal of continual prayer. The spirituality of ordinary lay people was a monastic spirituality; ordinary lay people expected to pray the daily offices, which means, of course, essentially to follow a liturgical life shaped by a regular, ordered rhythm—yearly, seasonal, daily."[23]

Similarly in the Middle Ages, the bells rang out from the spires of the magnificent medieval cathedrals, echoing high above the cities of Europe to form a prayer focus for the inhabitants. In the villages, homes nestled close around the parish church. Here too the bells beckoned the people to prayer and worship throughout the day, providing a sacred focus for the rhythm and pattern of their everyday activities. The church liturgical calendar provided a yearly cycle of activity, festivity, fasting, and rest that revolved around the life, death, and resurrection of Jesus, setting the pattern for the whole community's year.

Today too there are many people who have chosen to follow a different rhythm and who are good models or "life coaches" we can use to direct our paths. Don and Jocelyn Cowey were some of the first who provided this kind of example for me. Jocelyn is one of the most hospitable people I have ever met. She is always picking up strays and bringing them home for a meal. When I moved to Christchurch, New Zealand, as a young medical resident, I was one of those strays she met at church and invited to her home. I enjoyed the meal so much that a few weeks later I moved into their home as a boarder. In many ways she and her husband became family to me, supporting and encouraging me in faith and decisions throughout the years I spent in Christchurch. Today, twenty-five years later, they continue to provide an example for me and many others around the world.

Listen to the Beat—Following Our Life Coaches

John, a young pastor in Denver, told me about a recent conversation he had with a businessman in his congregation. "Why are you always so busy?" the businessman asked.

John, thinking his parishioner was looking for an accounting of his time, started to relate all the things he did that kept him constantly on the run—church commitments, committee meetings, family and friends, involvement in the community. The list was endless.

"No, no," the businessman exclaimed. "That's not what I meant. Why are you so busy all the time? Don't you think God wants you to model a different way of life?"

The question made John stop. He began rethinking his priorities and the pattern of his life.

The rhythm of life that Jesus and his disciples modeled throughout the New Testament is not just something for the dim dark distant past. It is a model that is meant to guide the pattern of our lives today. As the author of Hebrews reminds us, "Since we are surrounded by such a great cloud of witnesses, let us throw off everything that hinders and the sin that so easily entangles, and let us run with perseverance the race marked out for us" (Heb. 12:1). People today are looking to us for evidence that followers of Jesus have different priorities from the culture around them. They are looking for a faith with a different rhythm to life—a rhythm that is fulfilling instead of frustrating.

"Don't you think God wants you to model something different?" is *an important question that most of us need to think about seriously.* *So let's pull out our notebooks again and check our pulse:*

1. *Is your life in synch with the Jesus rhythm? List the aspects of Jesus' life and rhythm that you would most like to incorporate in your new rhythm of life.*
2. *Name several life coaches or role models with whom you most identify*
   a. from Christian history.
   b. from contemporary life.
3. *How would you like the rhythm of your life to look? Write a short paragraph that describes your ideal life based on the spiritual rhythms that you feel are most essential.*

3

PRACTICE MAKES PERFECT

*H*igh in the mountains of California stands a Russian Orthodox monastery without electricity, phones, or running water. Several years ago, John Marler, a young priest at the monastery and a former punk rocker, decided he wanted to reach out with the hope of Christ to the punk subculture from which he had escaped. He and his fellow monks decided to produce a 'zine. Called *Death to the World*, this rough homemade magazine is photocopied and offered cheap or free on the streets across the United States.[1]

"A typical flyer handed out to street kids, reads: 'Desert Wisdom Kaffe House, Kansas City's most mystical hangout. Drink Ethiopian coffee & espresso. Hear ancient other-worldly chants. Smell rare middle-eastern incense. Discover the ancient African & Eastern superheroes.' Of course the chants are Orthodox-style Christian hymns, the incense is borrowed from liturgical use, and the superheroes are saints of the Bible and church history."[2]

Since it was first published in 1994, the magazine has been a roaring success that has spawned coffeehouses or "mystical hangouts" across the United States, Europe, and Australia.

From Punk to Monk

What these Orthodox monks discovered does not surprise me. There is a growing spiritual hunger in the world. Wherever we travel, Tom and I encounter people from all traditions and walks of life who are searching, like these young punk rockers, for spiritual practices and religious routines that provide a more spiritually focused rhythm for their lives. Many are looking back to the monastic traditions of the past and to the life of Jesus and his early disciples. They are looking for creative ways to adapt these practices to the modern world. Others are experimenting with the routines and traditions of a variety of religions—Buddhism, Hinduism, and Islam to name a few. Still others are putting together their own religious patchwork quilt, drawing bits and pieces from various religions, cultures, and times, inventing their own form of spirituality as they go.

Most of us don't want to retreat to a monastery to find our rhythm, and I am not suggesting that any spirituality will do. As Christians we certainly don't want to invent forms that are not rooted in the values and beliefs of our faith. So what makes it possible for Christians to recognize God's rhythms, appreciate them, and desire to order our lives around them? It is one thing to listen to our life coaches and spiritual directors. It is another to put into practice what they tell us to do. How do we catch hold of that healthy rhythm modeled by Jesus and his disciples and bring it from the periphery of our overstressed and chaotic world to the center of all we are and do?

My own introduction to a life that is grounded in the rhythms and routines of the spiritual came through exposure to the monastic life, but in an unusual way. Brother Cadfael swept into my life as a "squat, barrel-chested, bandy-legged veteran of fifty-seven" when I first made his acquaintance in *A Morbid Taste for Bones,*[3] a medieval mystery set in 1137. As a Benedictine monk at the Abbey of Saint Peter and Saint Paul at Shrewsbury on the Welsh-English border, Brother Cadfael was part of an expedition into Wales to bring back the bones of Saint Winifred as patron saint for the abbey.

Brother Cadfael's life is modeled on that of a typical Benedictine monk of the twelfth century. Six times during the day and night the ringing of the bells called him to the chapter house for prayer and contemplation. As herbalist for the monastic community, he grew one of the best-stocked herb gardens in England, prepared his own medicines, and brewed his healing balms and syrups. Occasionally he ventured out into Shrewsbury to heal the sick.

Brother Cadfael was always something of a rogue and brought a certain earthiness and realism to his spiritual practices. The seat he selected in the chapter house was "well to the rear and poorly lit, half-concealed behind one of the stone pillars" so that he could be lulled to sleep, undetected, by the rhythmic reading of the psalms. On his forays into the outside world, as recorded in the nineteen books of *The Chronicles of Brother Cadfael,* he constantly tripped over dead bodies, puzzled out murders, and helped free those unjustly accused of crimes.

We can learn something from the life of my mythical friend. Cadfael came late to the monastic life. As an enthusiastic young man, he had joined the Crusades. For fifteen years he explored the world, roving as far afield as Venice, Cyprus, and the Holy Land, fighting in one campaign after another, first as a soldier and then as a sailor.

On his return to England, Cadfael's life changed. An encounter with God in a small parish church profoundly impacted him. He laid down his sword on the altar and decided to take the cowl instead. Despite his age and worldly experience, Cadfael took easily to the monastic life. He was "like a battered ship settling at last for a quiet harbour."

Brother Cadfael may be a mythical character, but his quest for a "quiet harbour" is no mythical quest. His discovery that the answer to this quest requires us to lay down our old life on the altar and take on a totally new life and rhythm is not mythical either.

The place that we all begin our search for a new rhythm that radiates out of our faith is at the foot of the cross of Christ. Here we lay down our old lives, our allegiances to the fast-paced, cyber-spaced consumer world, and literally take on the life of Christ and all the practices to which Christ calls us. Here we lay down the burdens of materialism, consumerism, and busyness that distract us from whole-hearted commitment to God. Here we reach out for the life that Christ offers us, a life of caring and compassion, of service to others, of resting in the closeness of God—the only rhythm that is truly satisfying.

Practicing the Rhythm

Like Cadfael, our spiritual journeys may begin with a sudden jolt—a blinding moment of revelation when we recognize our own sinfulness and reach out for the forgiveness that Christ offers through the cross. For others conversion may be a gradual transforming encounter. For all of us, however, it is not the act of conversion, important though it is, that will keep us on the right track for the rest of our lives. It is our continued allegiance to God, to God's kingdom, and to the new value system of love of God and neighbor that will enable us to grow into the richness and abundance of life Christ intends for us. The *spiritual practices and routines* we establish over time to *intertwine* our life story with the story of God in the long run provide a rhythm that will nourish us and grow our faith.

Jesus tells us, "Everyone who hears these words of mine *and puts them into practice* is like a wise man who built his house on the rock. The rain came down, the streams rose, and the winds blew and beat against that house; yet it did not fall, because it had its foundation on the rock" (Matt. 7:24–25, emphasis added). It is not just hearing the Word of God or even assenting to it in our minds that changes our lives—it is putting God's Word into practice and making it a rhythmic, vital part of our life story and our daily pattern.

In her book *Why Not Celebrate!* Sara Wenger Shenk says, "If it isn't possible to know the quickening presence of God in the everyday routine, one might as well ship religiosity off to a seminary library and leave it there. Either God is God of all of life, or God is on the reserve shelf, available and relevant only to a sanctified elite."[4] If our spiritual life does not provide rituals that punctuate our activities at regular intervals setting the rhythm for all we do, then we have relegated God to the reserve shelf and stored our faith away for emergency use only. To be a follower of Christ we must *intentionally work* to develop spiritual practices that put our faith and its rhythms at the *center* of all we are and do. Only then can we find a healthy life of stability and richness that easily withstands the pressures and stresses of our culture.

The Practice of Ritual

In the introduction to this book I suggested that the term *spiritual practice* refers to any routine or activity we perform regularly to deepen our intimacy with God. These practices provide the routines and rituals that undergird and reinforce our values and the principles by which we live. In the secular world there is a growing recognition of our need for spiritual practices and rhythms to help us cope with the escalating stresses of life. Martha Beck, a sociologist and professional life coach, admits, "I know that ritual is an incredibly powerful psychological process. . . . Modern Western culture has had most of the ritual stripped from it, leaving us less grounded and more alienated than many so-called primitive peoples. By putting ritual back into your life, you can help ease stress and enhance enjoyment, benefiting everything from *your immune system to your parenting skills, to your creativity*" (emphasis added).[5]

As urbanization slowly changed the face of our planet over the last two hundred years, religious routines weakened and spiritual practices and rituals were stripped away. We are all more stressed as a result. We are less healthy spiritually, emotionally, and physically. As the focal point of our communities moved from the village church to the city high-rise, with its office complexes and financial megaliths, the focus of our lives detached from the sacred rhythms of the monasteries and churches. We also disconnected from the religious events and festivals that gave spiritual significance to all our daily, weekly, and seasonal activities—no matter how mundane or unspiritual they may have seemed. In the process we threw out the spiritual rhythms through which we came face-to-face with the God who created our world and who gives rich purpose and abundance to all.

The spiritual rhythms of monastic communities revolved around the seasons and agricultural practices of people who paced their lives to the rhythm of the land. The rhythms of the land hold little relevance for people who live in the fast-paced urban world into which we were plunged by the industrial revolution. Our world's urban rhythms are totally disconnected from God's story, God's rhythms, and his purposes for our daily lives.

There is another reason for this disconnect. Since the Reformation, the Protestant church in the West has tended to look at ritual and liturgy with a disapproving eye. To many of us, fixed liturgical forms of worship are a recipe for boredom. To be honest, I am not surprised because many of the rituals of the church have become dead and meaningless to the average person. Author Rodney Clapp says the liturgy became extreme: "Like a prolific ivy in a tropical climate, liturgy had grown and spread and complicated itself until it was strangling or smothering everything around it. There was too much liturgy, and it was too ornate and complex for all but the ecclesiastical experts."[6]

Where Did We Go Wrong?

Tragically, we are not even aware of how this change has impacted us. Because the desire for rhythm and routine resides deep within our psyche, we don't give up on routines and rituals, we just change their focus. In the process we also change the focus of the underlying rhythms that pace our lives.

Today most of our daily activities and the rituals that give meaning to our lives are divorced from our religious experiences. Instead of revolving around the church, these rituals now emanate from the focal points of our urban centers—the secular workplace and consumer shopping mall. These tend to set the pace and rhythm of life and determine how we use our time and energy. The values that form the foundation for our rituals and habits are those of the global consumer culture not the values of our faith or God's kingdom. When our faith ceases to be the provider for these habits we must replace them with something, so we unconsciously but very effectively fill the void with the rhythms and addictive habits of our materialistic secular culture.

Since we like to avoid repetitive ritual, we feel that prayer and worship are more sincere and meaningful if the forms we use have never been seen or heard before. However, as Gertrud Mueller Nelson explains in her book *To Dance with God: Family Ritual and Community Celebration,* the lack of ritual and spiritual habits to shape our lives and undergird our activities has had dire consequences and our cure has sometimes been worse than the disease. "Rushing in to fill the void are the low-grade religious experiences which bedevil and taunt. We still search for meaning and the religious experience, but the powerful is more often encountered through the back door. Instead of having ritual ways to meet the awesome, we are overawed by our ritual habits, our fears and symptoms."[7]

We have replaced the holy fast of Lent with our spring diet obsessions prior to bathing suit weather. We shy away precipitously from community and the pain associated with carrying one another's burdens but exchange it for individualism and the agony of isolation and loneliness. Our days are no longer interrupted by times of nourishing spiritual reflections but by coffee breaks, aerobic workouts, and our favorite sitcom shows. We think we have escaped from the dead rituals of the past but are caught up instead in the compulsions of fashion fads, shopping sprees, and the allure of a new vitamin pill that promises healthy longer life. "Neurosis is the modern parody of religion and is the consequence of our lost orientation to the sacred."[8] No wonder our lives are unhealthy. Unless we can adopt rituals that deliberately remind us what it looks like to be a follower of Christ, we will never overcome our debilitating spiritual arrhythmias or break away from the unhealthy rhythms of our consumer culture.

The Power of Ritual

Have you ever noticed how much kids like to establish repetitive rituals for their daily activities? The slightest change to their morning routines can precipitate a tantrum akin to the breakout of World War III. Ritual and routine are powerful forces. They create fixed places—anchors to orient us, rhythms to give us structure for our daily duties, and symbols that provide meaning. They bring us into joyous relationship with God and enable us to discern his will. They nurture our personal healing processes and shape the communities in which we live and minister. In *Mighty Stories, Dangerous Rituals*, Herbert Anderson and Edward Foley express it this way: "Rituals are essential and powerful means for making the world a habitable and hospitable place. They are a basic vehicle for creating and expressing meaning. They are an indispensable medium by which we make our way through life."[9]

The incredible thing is that we don't have to settle for second best and succumb to the neurotic ritual fads of our culture. We have the unique opportunity to work creatively with God by developing rituals and routines that reflect God's kingdom values instead of those of the consumer culture. Gertrud Mueller Nelson says, "The making of ritual is a creative act fundamental in human life. It is also a divine gift."[10] Just as God brought order out of chaos in the creation story so we can use ritual and routine to bring order out of the chaos and confusion of our lives. In so doing we will create a world that is healthy and hospitable for us and others.

Of course this does not mean that all of our spiritual observances need to become ritualistic or liturgical in nature. Just as the seasons of the year provide a rhythmic structure within which there is room for infinite variety and creativity, so should our spiritual rhythms. There is room for the spontaneous and informal practices of our faith too. As Richard Foster says, "Both are inspired by the same spirit. We can be lifted into high, holy reverence by the richness and depth of a well-crafted liturgy. We can also be drawn into breathtaking wonder through the warmth and intimacy of spontaneous worship. Ours is a spirituality that can embrace both."[11]

As a keen gardener I can understand the need for balance between the ritualistic and the spontaneous in religious observances. Weeding, watering, and planting the garden in the proper seasons has forced me to develop routines or "rituals" at certain times of the year. After Christmas the seed catalogs arrive and I religiously pore over their tantalizing photos, trying to decide what I need for the coming spring. Then I start to plant. By the end of April our enclosed porch, which doubles as a greenhouse, looks like a tropical rainforest as I sprout lettuce, cabbages, and cauliflowers followed by tomatoes, squash, and peppers.

There are certain dates that any gardener in the Pacific Northwest keeps with religious fervor—peas go in the ground on President's Day; tomatoes, on Memorial Day; and autumn crops, the first week of June. Throughout the year there are weekly rituals of digging, fertilizing, and weeding that keep all of us busy until the harvest is ready to be picked.

Sometimes, however, I wander into the garden for the sheer joy of breathing the perfume of the roses or to appreciate the blossoming of my rather wild English country garden. However, I know that if these spontaneous trips were the only times I went into my garden, it would soon become an overgrown weed patch. Without the regular practices or rituals that provide the structure and shape for my garden, it would not be a garden. It would be a chaotic green mess.

Practicing Acts of Holy Imagination

Recognizing that we need ritual and routine to make life meaningful is one thing. Knowing how to connect these to our faith is another. Where do we start? In a recent sermon at St. Albans Episcopal Church, our rector, Dorsey McConnell, suggested we practice what he called "acts of holy imagination." By meditating on Scriptures such as the Sermon on the Mount, we can conjure an image of what a citizen of the kingdom of God looks like—a merciful compassionate caring peacemaker who is motivated by love for God and love of neighbor. We can then use this information to develop rituals that deliberately shape us so that we become more like the people God wants us to be.

I thought that was a wonderful idea. The place to start shaping a more spiritual rhythm to life is in prayer and meditation, imagining what we would be like if we were to become citizens of God's kingdom "transformed by the renewing of [our] minds" (Rom. 12:2). Then we can picture the rituals and habits we should develop so that our lives beat to the rhythms that governed Jesus' life—the rhythms of spiritual practice, work, rest, and community that we discussed in chapter 2. These are at the core of God's kingdom.

Imagine what our lives would be like if we practiced the values of God's kingdom. Imagine what our Christian communities would be like if we lived by the law of love for God and love of neighbor (Matt. 22:37–39). What practices should shape our days, weeks, and years to make this possible? As Christian anthropologist Paul Hiebert explains, "The answer to dead rituals is not no rituals but living rituals."[12] We need *living rituals* that are intentionally based on what it looks like to live as citizens of God's kingdom.

Spiritual Rhythms for Kingdom Living

Martha Beck gives three important pieces of advice when designing routines and rituals: *Keep it simple, stick to it, and make it meaningful.* We don't want practices that are burdensome. The idea is to design practices that enhance our lives without overwhelming us.[13] Let's focus on the four areas of our lives that need rituals in order to create the kind of balanced rhythm that Jesus lived by: our relationship to God, our emotional and spiritual states, our view of the world, and our rest and celebration. We will discuss these in more detail in subsequent chapters, but it is important to introduce them here.

First, we require practices that *intentionally* deepen our *relationship* to God—practices like daily prayer and Bible study, weekly church attendance and prayer gatherings. His intimate relationship to God made Jesus' single-minded purpose in life possible. A marriage or any relationship will falter and wither if it is not nurtured by adequate time spent together.

Second, we need practices that move us toward *wholeness and maturity,* and equip us to discover our calling as representatives of God's kingdom. Again prayer and Bible study are the mainstay of our development toward spiritual maturity. We will discuss this more in chapters 8 and 9. As we connect our lives to the events of Christ's life, death, and resurrection, we will find our pathway to healing and wholeness. Fasting, small group meetings, and annual prayer retreats to examine and refocus our direction are all possibilities that move us toward spiritual maturity. For example, Merrilee started a monthly Bible study with a group of women at her church to study the Scriptures and focus more intentionally on God's purposes.

Third, we need practices that *empower us to see beyond our own needs* to those of our hurting and broken world. We need rituals that intentionally focus our life on God's kingdom purposes, seeking to eradicate injustice and engender respect for all peoples. Sounds radical, I know, but sometimes this can be expressed in very simple ways. Greeting your colleagues at work with an enquiry about their health and their families lets them know you care. Honest concern is an expression of God's love. When I was in the hospital several years ago, I spent sleepless nights struggling with breathlessness and chest pains. One of the nurses visited me regularly, bringing a cup of tea—a ritual that is associated with comfort and caring in Australian culture. Her simple act expressed God's love to me in a way I will never forget.

We also need practices that consciously encourage us to serve others through hospitality, generous giving, and Christian service. Possibilities include buying a cup of coffee for a homeless person each week or carpooling with your neighbors in an effort to get to know them better.

Other simple rituals can revolve around our children's activities. Melanie takes her children to Pioneer Square in Seattle once a month so they can hand out lunches to homeless people. Keith and Marie sponsor children in a third-world country through World Vision. Their children, Brad and Matt, each have a sponsored child. Once a month the kids read letters from their sponsored friends and write replies. Susan and George go on an annual short-term missions trip to Mexico with their four kids. These situations provide opportunities for these families to model God's compassionate concern for the less privileged in our world. They encourage the children to move from the individualism of Western culture into the interdependence of the kingdom of God.

Fourth, we need practices that draw us into the *rest and the celebration of God's kingdom.* Consider how to establish rituals for Sabbath observances and retreat times. Think about taking pilgrimages to holy sites or sabbatical breaks. And don't forget to plan a party! We all need to celebrate the joy of God's presence, remembering that in enjoying each other we are enjoying God. Learning to party the story of God through the events of the liturgical calendar and celebrating the seasons of our lives are important practices that add richness and enjoyment to our faith. For example, Tom and I host an Advent party each year to celebrate the coming of Christ and the kingdom of God.

Of course we are not all drawn to the same types of practices. The idea of celebrating with a crowd may not excite you. In his book *Invitation to a Journey,* Robert Mulholland Jr. explains: "Each of us will tend to develop models of spiritual life that nurture our preference patterns. If extroversion is our dominant preference, we are going to select models of spirituality that bring us together with other people in worship, fellowship groups, prayer groups, Bible-study groups, spiritual formation groups. We will want corporate spirituality and will not get as much out of private, individualized spirituality. If our preference is introversion, we will adopt models of spirituality that emphasize solitude, reflection, meditation, contemplation. We will not get as much out of corporate experiences of spirituality as the extrovert."[14] Experiment a bit. Develop practices that are meaningful and appropriate for your personality.

A Place to Practice

Spiritual practices come in a variety of forms. Some require us to consciously set aside time and space just as Jesus did when he retreated into the hills to pray. A prayer room, a sacred garden, and a church sanctuary are all places that connect us to God. When we see our special place or enter it, we become calmer. Such places provide a haven of peace, an anchor for our souls in a chaotic world. Having a set time and place in which to meet God enriches prayer and worship.

Sometimes the use of symbols can help us make these places special or give them a sacred feel. Brother Andrew, author of *God's Smuggler,* set up a Bedouin tent in his prayer room as a reminder of the Arab people he prays for regularly.

Beth, who doesn't have lots of space, sits in the same chair each morning and lights a candle. The candle—symbolic of the presence of Christ, the light of the world—gives a focus to her morning prayer time. *Approaches to Prayer: A Resource Book for Groups and Individuals*[15] is an excellent resource for creating your own special prayer atmosphere; for example, lighting candles, listening to music or the sounds of nature such as a tape of water falling or birdsong, and using incense. The book contains suggestions to help individuals and groups.

Spiritual Practice and Daily Life—A Seamless Garment

In addition to having a special place in which to pray, other spiritual practices can be accomplished in the midst of our daily activities. Doing so brings a sense of the sacred into the most mundane activities. Jesus often prayed while preaching and healing, with hardly a pause between his words to God and those directed to his friends. We can enrich our lives with a sense of the sacred presence of God by saying grace before meals, reciting a short prayer of blessing before our children go to school or after we sit down at our desks at work, or playing Christian music in the background while preparing a meal or washing up. We can even invent prayers to use regularly before we turn on our computer, watch our favorite TV show, or attend a live sports event. When we do this, we consciously remind ourselves that these events are part of our Christian life rather than devoid of all spirituality. If you feel creative, you might like to invent your own celebration to commemorate the end of a work project or one for your children when they complete an arduous school assignment.

The early Celtic Christians were particularly aware of their interactions with God. They knew how to take the symbols of the culture around them and transform them into symbols of faith.

They even transformed the high places of the druidic worship into the high crosses of Christian worship. Esther de Waal says, "This is an approach to life in which God breaks in on the ordinary, daily, mundane earthy. It is very much a down-to-earth spirituality. The sense of the presence of God informs daily life and transforms it, so that any moment, any object, any job of work, can become the time and the place for an encounter with God."[16] She goes on to say that this sense of the spiritual provides a rhythm to life: "Here is a way of praying that is essentially holistic. I am reminded that as a human being living on this earth I am part of the pattern of day and night, darkness and light, the waxing and waning of the moon, the rising and setting of the sun. The whole of my self is inserted into the rhythm of the elements and I can here learn something, if I am prepared to, of the ebb and flow of time and of life itself."[17]

Celtic Christians had prayers for every daily activity —for kindling the fire in the morning, for milking the cow, and for planting the crops in the fields. They gave these mundane events spiritual significance. Kindling the fire each day mirrored the coming of the light of Christ into their lives. Three days before planting time they sprinkled the seed with water in the name of the Father, Son, and Holy Spirit. Seed was usually planted on a Friday, a symbol of Christ's death and burial and a reminder that Christ is the seed of the new world and of the resurrection. Here is one beautiful prayer for making the bed in the morning:

I make this bed
In the name of the Father, the Son and the Holy Spirit
In the name of the night we were conceived,
In the name of the night we were born,
In the name of the day we were baptized,
In the name of each night, each day,
Each angel that is in the heavens.[18]

In a more modern attempt to grapple with how to imbue the mundane with spiritual significance, Irish priest William Fitzgerald, in his book *Blessings for the Fast Paced and Cyberspaced*, suggests the use of blessing prayers. Drawing from his own Celtic background, he provides a wide range of prayers for activities such as opening e-mail, little league pilgrimages for dads and grandpas, and a trip to the mall. He even includes blessings to use when we are on the freeway and caught in a traffic jam—an event which we can transform from a time of fuming frustration and road rage into an opportunity to pray for the people in the cars around us. Here is one particularly delightful prayer about technology:

> O God, make my tools of technology into instruments of
> your peace today.
> May my cell phone connect me to blessings but disconnect
> me from trivia.
> May my automobile move me to safety, past road rage and
> road rush.
> May my e-mail enrich me with connectedness but also give
> me the wisdom to empty the trash.
> May the internet open up the world to me but not snare
> me into addictions.
> Through sights, sounds, movements and competition move
> my spirit on angels' wings.
> When day is done, may I come home again out of stress
> into peace and joy.[19]

Finding the Balance

Both these kinds of practices—those that require us to set aside special time and those that weave like a seamless garment through our everyday activities—are necessary for a healthy spiritual rhythm. Working together, they focus our lives on God and his values and enable us to make these our own. They provide the pivotal point for our spiritual rhythm and develop foundations that make it possible for us to grow and mature spiritually.

The Practice of Friends

Spiritual practices are not for isolated insulated individuals; they are one aspect of what binds us together in Christian community. Some practices we may do alone—such as daily prayer and Bible study. Others we can only effectively perform in a group—like worship, Christian service, and hospitality. Even those we do alone, however, connect us to others—to people who sing the same songs, pray the same prayers, and read the same Bible stories. Sometimes this sense of connectedness spans the globe or connects us back through two thousand years of Christian history. Whenever my husband, Tom, takes communion, he always feels a strong sense of connection to the many saints who have lived before us.

Quakers have produced a series of questions called *Queries* for silent contemplation that help believers focus on their shared faith. These are "thoughtful questions that remind people of the spiritual and moral values Friends seek to uphold." They cover the five areas that shape our lives—personal faith; the individual and the church; marriage, children, and home; manner of living; and concerns for society.[20] Terry Wallace says, "The Queries thus remind us that the church is not a spiritual supermarket with lots of spiritual fruit for sale in the produce section. They remind us we are not to wander up and down the aisles, testing each fruit to see if we should 'buy' it. . . . In hearing the Queries we are reminded of who we are as individuals and as the church—the people of God called to be a light to the world by letting our words *and* deeds proclaim the love, power and presence of Christ Jesus."[21]

As you develop your routines and practices, think about the community you identify with. How can you shape your rituals to increase your connectedness to that group and to the values they adhere to?

Listen to the Beat—Practicing the Rhythm

We truly are people of rhythm and ritual, and amazingly, through the power of God's spirit working in us, we hold within our grasp the possibility of shaping those rhythms and rituals in ways that intertwine our spiritual lives with everyday duties. We can take control of our lives and infuse them with rhythm that nourishes and maintains our faith and walk with God.

1. *What spiritual practices do you already incorporate in the rhythm of your life? Write down the spiritual routines and practices you perform on a regular daily, weekly, and yearly basis that provide rhythm for your life.*
2. *How would you like to change the rhythm of your life to make it more focused on the values of your faith? Write a short paragraph outlining the ways in which you would like to see your spiritual rhythm changed.*
3. *What new spiritual practices would you like to incorporate on a regular daily, weekly, or yearly basis to reach your goals?*

4

CATCH THE RHYTHM

*T*he Pirahã people of Brazil are always singing. Kids sing as they play, women sing as they work, and men sing to the spirits at night. They communicate through their own unique form of "sung-speech," which for them has far more meaning than spoken speech. When Wycliffe Bible translators Dan and Keren Everett were translating the story of the ailing woman who touched the hem of Jesus' robe, the Pirahã woman working with them spontaneously began retelling the story in Pirahã sung-speech. Suddenly people started to gather, and the house soon filled with villagers eager to hear the story. For the first time they heard the gospel story conveyed in their cultural way of sharing spiritual information. The story of Jesus finally came to life.[1]

Singing New Songs

Many of us feel that we are practicing our faith with rituals and routines that are meaningless. We need to sing new songs like the Pirahã people, so the gospel story comes to life again. Finding meaningful ways to pray, worship, and reach out to people in our urban world is not always easy. Although our lack of spiritual rhythms may not be obvious to us, it is often blatantly obvious to others. People of other cultures have always been unimpressed by the spirituality of North American and European Christians and by the way we allow the secular culture to set our pace and rhythms.

In her book *Walking on Water,* Madeleine L'Engle quotes Alice Kaholusana, a Hawaiian Christian: "Before the missionaries came, my people used to sit outside their temples for a long time meditating and preparing themselves before entering. Then they would virtually creep to the altar to offer their petitions and afterwards would again sit a long time outside, this time to 'breathe life' into their prayers. The Christians, when they came, just got up, uttered a few sentences, said AMEN and were done. For that reason my people called them 'haoles,' [people] 'without breath,' or those who failed to breathe life into their prayers."[2]

In a similar vein, a missionary to Ghana in West Africa recently told me that she was horrified to hear that the local African Christians never invited the missionaries to their prayer meetings. The African experience had led them to believe that westerners did not really trust in the power of prayer except for very spiritually focused purposes. They handed out pills and medical treatment or gave advice on how to plant crops and make money instead.

Where do we look for those life-giving rituals we so desperately need to connect our daily activities to our faith? How can we catch a new rhythm that breathes life into all we do?

Breathing Life into Our Journey

A couple of years ago, I searched for resources to help me develop practices that intentionally connect me to God and his purposes. In my quest I discovered a number of recent books about people's hunger for spiritual rhythm. Kathleen Norris's best-seller *The Cloister Walk*,[3] in which she describes her extended time in a monastery, is an example of a contemporary book that shows how liturgy, ritual, and a sense of community can impart meaning to everyday events. The Northumbria Community's *Celtic Daily Prayer*[4] is another excellent resource that connects to the Celtic tradition and uses the daily offices as a guide for prayer. Unfortunately these books often require a leisurely way of life to effectively put their recommendations into practice. They offer little help for those who live in urban mega-cities and move to a fast-paced 24/7 beat. In this chapter we will address this challenge and grapple with the types of rituals and spiritual practices we need to give our fast-paced lives shape and meaning.

The Power to Restore and Transform

Christian anthropologist Paul Hiebert talks about two types of spiritual rituals that ground us in the principles of faith. These hold the key to new rhythms. The first and by far the most common is the *ritual of restoration*. "In this type of ritual, people gather to restore their faith in the beliefs that order their lives, and to rebuild the religious community in which these beliefs find expression."[5] The second type of practice is what Dr. Hiebert calls *rituals of transformation*. These provide a structure that enables us to bring change into our lives. Hiebert explains that these rituals "are characterized by a high degree of creativity and antistructure. . . . They cut through the established way of doing things and restore a measure of flexibility and personal intimacy."[6]

The Rhythm of Restoration

During World War II thousands of European children were orphaned and left to starve. Many ended up in refugee camps where they were given food and care. At night they often couldn't sleep because they were afraid they would wake up homeless and starving again. Eventually someone gave each child a piece of bread to hold at bedtime—and they finally slept through the night in peace. This simple ritual reassured these refugee children that just as they had been fed today, so they would be fed tomorrow.[7]

We may not want to take a loaf of bread to bed with us, but we all need simple restorative rituals that regularly reassure us of the precepts of our faith and provide us with security and stability. Reciting simple prayers with your children before they go to bed at night is a great way to establish this same kind of security. I guarantee that it is something they will remember for the rest of their lives. The more uncertain our lives and the more chaotic and changeable the world around us, the more we need the stability of daily spiritual practices and weekly worship to maintain our equilibrium.

Restorative spiritual practices are highly structured and should not change from day to day or from year to year. Because we repeat them regularly, they reaffirm our sense of order and meaning in our lives. We need stable spiritual rituals to anchor our lives and give them meaning. If our daily prayers are random and unstructured or if we church hop every week and don't establish regular spiritual routines, our whole life suffers.

Restorative spiritual practices should travel with us wherever we go. Our society is highly mobile. The average family moves every two years, and this can destabilize us. Moving strips away our anchors and our sense of belonging. Establishing spiritual routines for kids when we move provides security and may be more important than finding a good school.

Restorative spiritual practices should be tailored to our needs. Eydie and Greg, who have moved several times in the last few years, tell me that with two kids under five, they need short family rituals—thirty seconds or less—to maintain their stability. One good resource they discovered is *Thank You for This Food* by Debbie Trafton O'Neal. It provides some wonderful prayers, songs, and mealtime blessings for kids with actions included. One of their favorites is "Lord bless this bunch as we crunch our lunch! Amen."[8] At bedtime they conclude their children's prayers with these words from the *Book of Common Prayer:* "Lighten our darkness, we beseech thee, O Lord; and by thy great mercy defend us from all perils and dangers of this night; for the love of thy only Son, our Savior, Jesus Christ." Their children, Jackie and Brendan, have already memorized the words.

This does not mean, however, that our prayers and spiritual observances need to become monotonous and boring, nor does it mean they should never change. Within the patterns we establish there should be room for creative new expressions in response to changes in our careers, family situations, or life stages. Various events shape our spiritual routines and require us periodically to restructure them. Our religious affiliation, cultural heritage, personality, and experiences also influence the spiritual routines we develop.

Rhythms of the World

"Show your faith in the new millennium—buy a calendar" proclaimed a sign at our local mall. The world around us abounds with advice on restorative rituals designed to reinforce our faith in the values of its super malls and the frenetic pace of life it propounds. Trekking to fabulous fall sales, using aromatherapy oils to cheer our holiday gatherings, getting hourly stock market updates on CNN, and watching our favorite weekly TV show are all rituals we may unconsciously have that reinforce our beliefs in the consumer culture and its applause for self-gratification.

The rituals we unconsciously teach our kids are even more focused on the high-paced cyber beat of the secular world and dramatically reflect the values of the consumer religion we worship. The once-slow rhythm of family meals that revolved around prayer and fellowship have been replaced by a weekly mad dash to "You deserve a break today" McDonald's for the latest Happy Meal and its accompanying Disney cartoon toy. The former family rituals of outings to the park, woods, or creek that taught kids to appreciate the beauty of God's creation have been replaced by trips to the mall for the latest must-have book or toy and frantic races across town to the next soccer practice.

Not all secular rituals are bad, however, as Tom and Valerie Norwood discovered when they took their youth group skiing. On the way home, they stopped at Krispy Kreme Doughnuts although the queue stretched around the building, forcing them to stand in the bitterly cold weather for half an hour. Through the glass display window they watched the doughnuts drop into the boiling fat and slide along their greasy path until they were cooked. Then the machine flipped them into the sugar and cinnamon mix and poured them in boxes that the young people grabbed eagerly. They sat around the crowded tables devouring their doughnuts with religious fervor. It was such a great friendship-building event that they started a ritual. Future skiing trips will include a stop for doughnuts.

Restorative Rhythms to Live By

Tom and I learned to appreciate the refreshing power of restorative faith-based rituals when we began attending an Episcopal church in Seattle. Every week we recite the same prayers and sing the same songs affirming our faith. I did not grow up in a liturgical church, so at first I found this challenging. However, as I memorized the prayers and allowed them to resonate deep within my soul, I found the worship more and more enriching. Now I crave the order and repetition. Such order provides an oasis of rest in the midst of my busy life.

I am also awed that I worship not only with our own small congregation but also with millions of others around the world who use these same prayers each week. No matter where we travel in the world we find churches that use the same formats. With knowledge of shared liturgy, we instantly bond to new members of God's family. Since faithful followers of Christ have prayed these same prayers over the centuries, I gain a calming sense of continuity and stability in the midst of today's highly mobile society.

You may not be attracted to a liturgical church, but you might want to consider establishing your own restorative rituals by regularly repeating some simple prayers or Scripture readings. Our good friend Tom Balke, who attends a Mennonite Brethren church, uses the Jesus Prayer—"Lord Jesus Christ, Son of God, have mercy on me, a sinner"—as a restorative ritual. "It is a prayer that is in synch with whom God created me to be," he told me. For Tom, too, the feeling of connection to Christians who prayed this prayer throughout the history of Christianity brings a welcome sense of renewal.

How *protective* are you of your daily prayer and Bible study habits and your weekly church attendance? What do you do on a regular basis to *reaffirm* your faith and *reconnect* to a larger religious community? Unless we can adopt rituals that deliberately remind us what it looks like to be a follower of Christ, we will never break away from the unhealthy rhythms of our consumer culture.

Creating a New Pattern

Since I recognized the power of regular restorative practices, I have worked hard to develop a pattern that connects my daily spiritual observances to the rhythm of my life. I wrote down the characteristics of my faith that needed reinforcing and divided them into seven themes—one for each day of the week. These now form focal points for my daily devotions. To sharpen my focus I purchased a loose-leaf notebook and divided it into seven sections—one for each day of the week. Each section begins with Scriptures that reflect my theme. To these I added ideas and quotes from my Bible and other spiritual books or from the Sunday sermon.

I read these verses and quotes first thing in the morning. They make good meditation points. Then as I read the newspaper I write down prayer points that connect to that day's theme and use these as a focus for my prayer time. I devised questions that encourage me to incorporate this theme into my day's activities.

Monday, I focus on God the Creator, creativity, and the call to be stewards of God's creation. Sometimes I start the day by reflecting on how God is revealed in creation through the rhythm of the day and year or through the beauty and majesty of all created things. On occasion I meditate on God's creativity expressed in the rich diversity and incredible complexity of life around me and contemplate the creativity I see in human endeavors such as fashion or architectural design. I use this as a launching point to think about my life and how God could use my creativity in the coming day. My questions for the day are either "In what ways am I called to steward God's creation today?" or "How will my actions today glorify God's creative work in the world?" I focus my prayers on those impacted by environmental disasters, on creation care ministries, and on those engaged in creative arts. As a result, I find myself praying for farmers and landscape gardeners, for fashion designers and environmentalists—people I was hardly aware of before.

Tuesday, I focus on Christ our Savior and what it means to bear his image into the world. I reflect on ways that I can model Christ to others and think about how those around me reveal Christ to me. I pray for those who seek to be an incarnation of Christ to people who live in poverty, despair, or oppression—particularly for situations I have read about in the newspaper during the week. I ask, "How can Christ-in-me show forth his love and compassion in my actions today?" and "In what ways do the faces of my family, friends, and those I pass in the street reflect the image of God?" Asking these questions has totally changed my attitude toward work and my community. Grocery shopping is no longer just to buy food; it is an opportunity to interact with people for whom God cares and Christ died.

Wednesday, I focus on the Holy Spirit and my need to be equipped as God's servant. Sometimes I start the day by reading my mission statement—"To be a voice for those who have no voice and bring glimpses of God's shalom kingdom into people's lives." I ask, "How can I live this out in my life today?" or "How do I need to be better equipped to be God's voice for the voiceless?" Then I strategize about practical ways in which I can apply my ideas. I pray for places in which I can see the Holy Spirit at work, places where there are indications of renewal like the emerging postmodern church movement.

Thursday, I turn my focus toward community. I think about what it means to be part of God's worldwide community and how that oneness can be expressed through hospitality and compassionate care to others. I reflect on God's international community and pray for those who suffer from hunger, poverty, disease, or injustice. Sometimes I ask myself, "What do I plan to do today that will help build God's community?" I also ask, "How will I help draw others into God's community today?" Sometimes I focus on a far more difficult question: "In what ways do I discriminate against others who are part of God's community?" I pray for those who suffer from AIDS and other devastating diseases, for those who are persecuted because of their faith, and for those who are discriminated against because of race, color, age, disabilities, or gender. This has made me very aware of the diversity of the human race. It has also opened my eyes to the rich variety of ways God reveals himself through different cultures.

Friday, not surprisingly, is my day to reflect on the cross of Christ and the wholeness God brings through restoration and reconciliation. Sometimes I pray about where I still need to be restored, or I ask God's forgiveness for the obstacles that keep me from a whole-hearted commitment to Christ. I like to ask, "In what ways do I need to lay down my life today and intentionally embrace the life of Christ?" Sometimes I ask more difficult questions: "Are there areas of sin that I need to confess or people I need to be reconciled to?" I pray for countries torn apart by conflict and war and for those I know who work in ministries of reconciliation and peacemaking.

Saturday, I reflect on God's kingdom and the "cloud of witnesses" who have gone before me. I love to read stories about followers of Christ who dared to be different and lived as citizens of God's kingdom. I gain confidence as I connect my own sense of purpose to the wonderful examples of Christians who have lived valiantly over the last two thousand years. My questions revolve around my call to be a witness. I ask, "How can I live today as a testimony to God?" I pray for missionaries and mission organizations I am involved in that reflect glimpses of God's shalom kingdom.

Sunday is a day to celebrate the resurrection and the new life we receive through salvation. I rejoice in being a new creation in Christ and focus on the wonder of that new life. My questions are "What am I most grateful for this week?" and "What have I accomplished this week that reflects my new life in Christ and bears the seal of God's approval?"

This exercise has greatly enriched my spiritual life and intentionally enabled me to integrate my daily routines with my Christian faith. I am amazed at the joy this has brought me. For example, focusing on God's creativity made me realize that I too could be creative. I started writing poetry, something that would never have occurred to me before. I wrote the following poem one morning while reflecting on God's beauty as revealed in the rising sun.

> I awake this day to the joy of life
> A sudden sunrise, a royal pageant,
> Red and gold splashed across the sky
> Like the daybreak of your light
> It penetrates the darkest gloom
> God-in-me vibrant colors shining through.
> Sometimes black clouds obscure your brightness
> Roaring thunder, jagged lightning
> Clinging sin lances through my soul
> It waits for the deluge of your grace
> The cleansing rain that purifies my life
> Forgiving love, embracing care
> God-in-me muted colors waiting patiently.

I have also tried to connect these themes to my other daily activities. I love to walk, and I constantly look for creative ways to use my spiritual themes in my daily walks. Monday, I focus on my enjoyment of God's creation. There is a lake five minutes from our home with a three-mile walking track around it where I love to go to soak in the beauty of God's creation. Sometimes Tom and I walk around our neighborhood admiring the gardens. We are reminded that the first responsibility God entrusted to humans was to steward creation and make it flourish. Our walks encourage us to pray for all who are involved in creation care. Tuesday as I walk I think about how the face of Christ is reflected in the countenances of people I pass. Wednesday, I like to walk the neighborhood, asking God's Spirit to open my eyes so that I can discern the needs and dreams of my community.

Living on Purpose

Matthew, who works in downtown Los Angeles, adapted these same themes for use during lunchtime as a way to connect more intentionally to the downtown area. Monday, he eats in a local park—even when it rains! He spends a few minutes meditating on God revealed in creation—through the changing patterns of the seasons and through the beauty and diversity around him. "Rain is no longer an inconvenience that makes the roads slippery," he says. "It is a reminder of the refreshment and renewal God's cleansing brings into all our lives."

His ventures outside are probably good for his health too. Research suggests that for those who spend long hours in artificially lighted and temperature-controlled environments exposure to creation is not just good for our spirits, it is also good for our bodies. We are less likely to suffer from allergies, insomnia, depression, and the effects of seasonal affective disorder if we have regular interaction with nature.

Breakfast with Friends

On Tuesday Matthew uses the story of Jesus' breakfast on the beach with his friends as a model. He reasons that if Jesus could take time out of his busy schedule to spend with his friends then so can he. He arrives early at work with doughnuts, muffins, and coffee for his colleagues. No meeting is involved; it is just a time for everyone to get to know each other. In the months since he began serving this treat, Matthew has learned much about his friends' hopes and dreams. Now when someone has a problem they come to Matthew because they know he cares and prays for them.

On Wednesday Matthew prayer-walks the neighborhood, asking God to open his eyes and give him God's compassion for the community. On Thursday he catches up on errands that get him out of his office into the neighborhood. Matthew loves to talk to the people he meets—shop owners, tenants, homeless people, urban ministry people. He deliberately shies away from ATM machines or drive-through windows because he believes that developing relationships is far more important than saving a few minutes.

Interacting with bank tellers, shop assistants, and fast food vendors may be one way that you can establish Christ's presence in your neighborhood. So many of us are disconnected from the communities where we work. We need to gain a sense of God's presence in these "second homes" we inhabit eight hours or more a day.

Friday for Matthew is an open day to spend with a colleague or at one of the local homeless shelters. On Saturday his family works in a community project or urban mission. Something as simple as organizing a neighborhood watch or volunteering for an hour at the local food bank or picking up trash in the local park may be a way to purposefully connect your spiritual observances to ministry in your neighborhood.

Rituals of Change

I am a science fiction buff and a lover of mystery stories, so you can imagine my delight when I discovered a novel that combined mystery, murder, and interstellar intrigue. *Hellspark* by Janet Kagan is set in a future in which humankind has established new worlds and cultures throughout the galaxy. The book tells the story of Tocohl Susumo, a Hellspark trader who goes to the newly discovered planet of Lassti to help a friend. What follows is a wonderful interplay of crosscultural misunderstandings, conflict, and mayhem as Tocohl judges the disputes of the intergalactic scientific team that is investigating the planet.

At one point in the story, it is absolutely essential that a male member of the team, swift-Kalat, speak to Layli-LayliCalulan, a woman from the planet Yn. She is in mourning for her murdered husband and in her culture speaking to a man at this time is strictly taboo. In a brilliant piece of strategy Tocohl invents what she calls the "Hellspark ritual of change."⁹ She waves her hands over swift-Kalat, says "Hey presto," and symbolically changes him into a woman. The two are able to talk, the crisis is resolved, and the murder is solved. Later we discover that the other team members take this new ritual very seriously. What she has created is not just a make-believe ceremony but a powerful tool that has the possibility of bringing major change to the cultures of planets across the galaxy.

The Power to Transform

In the real world too, rituals of transformation—or as the Hellsparks called it, "rituals of change"—are powerful tools because they allow us to embrace and accept change without being overwhelmed or disrupted by it. Transformational rituals include spiritual practices such as prayer retreats, pilgrimages to holy sites, spiritual growth conferences, special revival services, and religious festivals. On the individual and family level they include rites of passage such as baptism, confirmation, birthdays, marriage, death, and other transitions in life.

Have you noticed how our modern culture loves to fashion rituals to transform and renew us? It persuades us to buy a bigger car and a more expensive house to go with our job promotion. Ads, the purveyors of change, condition us to believe that updating our computers and technological gadgets every couple of years is essential to keep abreast of the rapidly changing technology. Recently I came across a snow-globe phone that celebrates the seasons with four interchangeable handsets so that you can swoosh down the ski slopes in winter, take a hot air balloon ride in spring, swim at the beach in summer, and bike through the falling leaves in autumn—all while talking to friends from the comfort of your living room.

Fashion fads too condition us to discard our old wardrobe each season and reach for a new set of clothes. Tom told me that when he lived in Hawaii the kids felt a strange compulsion to keep up with the seasonal fashion trends dictated by the mainland culture. In the middle of winter—80 degrees and above there—they purchased heavy down parkas from the frigid north and walked around in their own personal saunas for the next few months. Though we don't recognize it, our culture has rituals designed to conform our behavior to the changing values of our cyber world rather than to our biblical faith.

Moving the Ark

I learned a deep appreciation for transformative spiritual rituals during my years on the *Anastasis* where life constantly changed as we moved from port to port. Each time the ship prepared to sail, we held what we called a "moving of the ark" ceremony, based on our understanding of the ark of the covenant. The ark contained the law given to Moses on Mount Sinai and symbolized God's presence with the Israelites in the wilderness. The cloud of God's presence hung over it by day, and a flame of fire burned over it at night. The people journeyed only when the cloud moved. When the cloud stopped they set up camp again.

Similarly, for us on the ship, there was a strong sense that we only wanted to move when God moved. We celebrated with a special worship service that brought us together for a time of reflection and preparation. Sometimes we needed a time of repentance, reconciliation, and forgiveness before we could participate in communion. We ended with an exuberant worship service, looking ahead to the next port with its challenges and opportunities.

Now that I live in a house that doesn't move every few months, I have had to rethink my transformative rituals. Three or four times a year Tom and I go on a prayer retreat. We take a couple of days to get away to refocus and check in with God. Sometimes we combine these retreats with pilgrimages to holy sites like the island of Iona off the west coast of Scotland. This small island was one of the first monastic sites for the Celtic Christians and has become a popular site for pilgrims of faith. On other occasions Tom and I book a room in a local hotel to get away from our house, jobs, and distractions. These retreats have become some of our best prayer times. They provide stability and continuity in the midst of rapid change.

Developing ceremonies and rituals like these keep us flexible and provide the creativity we need to grow spiritually and resist the pressures of secular culture. Such rituals encourage us periodically to rethink and reshape our life rhythms, especially when we face major changes or life passages—like when we get a new job, move to a new city, or become empty nesters. This helps us take charge and direct what change we allow into our lives so that we no longer "conform to the pattern of this world," but are instead "transformed by the renewing of our minds" (Rom. 12:2).

Researching Three Areas

Where do we look for practices that breathe life not only into our prayers but also into everything we do? How do we find rituals that reinforce our faith in God and his values rather than in the liturgies of image and status of our consumer culture?

I think we can learn a lesson from the Girl Scouts. They constantly research the culture and have developed an incredible array of ritual practices designed to help young women cope with current cultural pressures. The Stress Less badge, embroidered with a swinging hammock, is one recent addition introduced to reduce stress. One troop in Sunnyvale, California, organized a stress clinic for third-grade Brownies that included the troop's favorite aromatherapy massage lotion recipe.[10]

We too need to do research in three areas before we plan our restorative and transformative rituals. First, we should choose the faith values we want to shape our lives. Perhaps, like me, you want to develop themes for each day of the week. Think about your life and mission. What spiritual themes would you like to reinforce each week? How could you connect these to your daily activities? Enlist the aid of a mentor or friend. Sit down with a big piece of paper and do some brainstorming. Discuss your life passions and get creative.

Second, we need to research the culture and the values it propounds, so we can stand against the harmful ones. A growing number of youth churches are taking up this challenge and incorporating practices into their worship services that help young people decode the values of the consumer culture. For several weeks before the Emmy awards, Centrepoint, a young people's church in Grand Rapids, Michigan, uses the songs nominated for awards as the focus for their worship. They help their members unpack the good, the bad, and the ugly in the songs. They enable them to think about the messages behind the lyrics—the emphasis on sex and drugs, the overvaluation of body image, the themes of hopelessness and despair. In the process the church helps the young people connect to themes from the biblical story—to the themes of hope and redemption that often stand in stark contrast to the themes of secular music.

Third, we need to research possible rituals and routines to incorporate into our lives. According to Anderson and Foley, the use of ritual "helps create a sense of continuity in our lives by linking the past to the present and the present to the future. In the midst of life's discontinuities, rituals become a dependable source of security and comfort."[11] By linking the past to the present through rituals, we give ourselves a wonderful sense of continuity to carry into the future. This helps strengthen our faith and enables us to adhere to our spiritual beliefs in spite of cultural pressures.

Rooted in the Past

The place to start creating that sense of continuity is by researching the rich heritage of religious practices that permeate every Christian tradition. There are already more church rituals, blessings, and festivities in existence than we could relate to in a lifetime. We may have to dig to find them, or they may be right in front of us. There are blessings for starting the day and ending it, blessings for a new house and a new baby, blessings for the harvest and for the fishing fleet, blessings for the major events in life as well as the everyday and mundane. There is even a blessing for beer![12] We can also look at the cultural heritages of our families, our communities, and the Jewish faith from which many Christian practices emerged. These traditions all provide strong anchors that stabilize us during life's storms. What practices from the lives of the early disciples, from your own faith tradition, or from the heritage of others would you like to introduce into your life to help develop spiritual focus?

Incorporating the past in our spiritual rituals enables us to gain perspective on our present situation and feel connected to the overarching biblical story. Knowing we have a heritage gives us a powerful sense of God's faithfulness in the past and an empowering confidence in God's future leading. As God reminded the Israelites, "Only be careful, and watch yourselves closely so that you do not forget the things your eyes have seen or let them slip from your heart as long as you live. Teach them to your children and to their children after them" (Deut. 4:9).

When I was writing my book *Tales of a Seasick Doctor*,[13] in which I share my adventures during twelve years on board the mercy ship *Anastasis*, I spent many wonderful evenings with friends, reflecting on our years together. One evening we reminisced and shared stories about God's faithful and sometimes miraculous provision. The next day a friend who hadn't been with us asked, "What on earth did you talk about last night? Everyone was walking around on cloud nine this morning." Reminiscing about God's faithfulness in the past refreshed us and reinforced our ability to trust in God for the present. Unfortunately the busier our lives become the harder it is to find time to reflect on the past and the wonderful faithfulness of God. It is even harder to find time to share these reflections with our children and grandchildren.

An Eye on the Future

In addition to connecting to our heritage, we need to look ahead and develop practices that connect us to God's will for the future. Jeremiah reminds us, "'I know the plans I have for you,' declares the Lord, 'plans to prosper you and not to harm you, plans to give you a hope and a future'" (Jer. 29:11). The Old and New Testaments are alive with beautiful and compelling imagery of God's future, but few of us are aware of this imagery. We rarely use it as a focus for our lives and activities. Knowing God is in control of the future gives hope that enriches and stabilizes in amazing ways.

We also need rituals that make us aware of how our world is changing and how God expects us to be involved in making a difference in that world. Spiritual rituals are not just to help us cope with the present. They are particularly helpful in enabling our children to prepare for the future world in which they will live. In *Mustard Seed vs McWorld*, my husband, Tom Sine, looks at some of the challenges likely to impact us in the future. He mentions the responsibility we have to the next generation: "Those of us who are parents, grandparents, pastors, educators, and youth workers have a special responsibility to equip the young for life in a demanding future. . . . I believe we are often doing the opposite of what we should be doing to equip our young people to live, thrive and serve God in a new millennium."[14]

Equipping our young people and ourselves for the future is not an easy task, but it is even harder if we pay no attention to how that future will look. Developing practices that enable us to be proactive rather than reactive will relieve current and future stresses.

What practices will enable us to cope effectively in a rapidly changing world? How can we foster the family and community relationships necessary to deal with the increasing stress and chaotic change ahead of us? Above all how can we develop practices that connect our lives and the lives of future generations to God, that unchangeable vision that gives such hope and encouragement for the future?

Anchored in the Present

While we remember our heritage and ponder the future, we should also evaluate our present habits and rituals—those that connect us to God, move us toward personal wholeness, and connect us to the needs of our families, communities, and world. Which of these habits already have the signature of God stamped on them? How can we preserve these practices and the rhythm they provide? Gardening is an important part of my rhythm that brings both renewal and refreshment. When I am irritable or disgruntled, an hour in the garden transforms me. Tom says that my face glows when I come inside.

It wasn't an accident that God created humankind in a garden. What a garden it was! Every conceivable plant and animal coexisted in rich harmony. The air pulsed with melodies of dazzling birds, and heady perfume of roses tantalized the senses. Lush fruit and rich grassland provided food for zebras, giraffes, kangaroos, and every other imaginable animal. God placed humanity in the midst, not just to enjoy the garden but to "work it and take care of it" (Gen. 2:15). Incredibly we get the impression that God spent time in the garden too, walking with humankind and drinking in the beauty of creation (Gen. 3:8).

Celebrating God's presence in the garden is one way I absorb the soothing rhythms encased in the seasons of the year. I was delighted therefore when I discovered gardening always had an important place in monastic life. In *A Monastic Year: Reflections from a Monastery,* Brother Victor-Antoine d'Avila-Latourrette explains the link between gardening and spiritual rituals: "At the beginning of time, gardening was recognized as part of God's mandate to man to care for the Earth. The early monks in the Egyptian desert took to heart this Biblical command, becoming avid gardeners as well as watchful stewards of the land entrusted to them. The idea of the garden was dearly loved by them, for it also enabled them to recreate the paradise man and woman once shared with God."[15]

Listen to the Beat—Catch the Rhythm

Many rituals in our lives already bear the signature of God—and sometimes even the most unexpected aspects of who we are and what we do carry God's seal of approval. What an incredible joy it is to discover this. For example, Ev has always loved to paint, but as a young person making a vocational decision she did not feel that art was a good job for a Christian. However, as her faith matured, Ev realized that our creator God has called all of us to express our creative gifts. She has not only taken up painting again but also gives art lessons to other budding artists. Her once despised gift obviously bears God's seal of approval and has brought great joy and satisfaction to her life.

Ian works at a waste treatment plant. He always felt embarrassed to admit this to his friends. Then he discovered that responsibility for sanitation in ancient Israel belonged to the Levites—the priests. It transformed his view of his profession. Now he realizes that this once embarrassing job is really a priestly calling that carries God's approval.

When we connect the routines and rhythms that shape our lives to this journey, we can embrace all God intends for us. In the process we find satisfaction and enrichment.

What spiritual practices and habits would you like to shape your life?

1. *Write a short paragraph that describes the restorative practices that shape your life. Which of these are rooted in the values of your faith and which reinforce the values of the consumer culture?*
2. *What routines in your life initiate or encourage change? How could you reinforce and preserve those practices that are rooted in your faith?*
3. *What new restorative and transformative practices would you like to establish to help provide a rhythm to your life that flows out of your faith?*

5

PRESCRIPTION
FOR A HEALTHY LIFE

*D*uring my early days on the *Anastasis* in Greece, we often struggled with lack of money as the renovation of this old ship inched toward completion. In our desperation we decided to do what Jesus did. We called for forty days of prayer and fasting to focus on God's will for the ministry's future. We encouraged members of the community to pray and fast for several days over this time span. Each morning we met for prayer in a room that looked out over the Mediterranean Sea.

One morning at the end of the forty days, I was standing at the back of the room gazing at the sea when I noticed flashes of silver, like sunlight reflected in a mirror, erupting from the water. The flashes cascaded onto the beach in a brilliant stream of light. Suddenly a ripple of excitement spread across the room. "The fish are jumping!" someone shouted, and we all raced outside to witness the amazing display. In front of our hotel there were fish literally throwing themselves out of the water onto the beach. Some leaped high into the air before they landed at our feet. Others flopped in exhausted puddles around us. They lay stranded, in gasping wriggling heaps all along the water's edge.

We collected 8,301 fish that morning. It seemed miraculous. We sang and rejoiced, marveling at the incredible way God answered our prayers. None of us had expected anything so dramatic or unusual. We felt the assurance of God's continued presence with us, and it gave us new hope for the future.[1]

Prescription for Prayer

Most of us believe in the power of prayer and are convinced that we should study the Scriptures regularly, but how many of us are as surprised as we were in Greece when God answers? Few of us approach our prayers and Scripture study with the passion and conviction that the psalmists expressed when they came to God.

> O God, you are my God,
>   earnestly I seek you;
> my soul thirsts for you,
>   my body longs for you,
> in a dry and weary land
>   where there is no water.
>
> I have seen you in the sanctuary
>   and beheld your power and your glory.
> Because your love is better than life,
>   my lips will glorify you.

I will praise you as long as I live,
and in your name I will lift up my hands.
My soul will be satisfied as with the richest of foods;
with singing lips my mouth will praise you.

Psalm 63:1–4

Oh, how I love your law!
I meditate on it all day long.
Your commands make me wiser than my enemies, for they
are ever with me.
I have more insight than all my teachers, for I meditate on
your statutes. . . .
How sweet are your words to my taste, sweeter than honey
to my mouth! . . .
Your word is a lamp to my feet and a light to my path.

Psalm 119:97–99, 103, 105

It is hard to distinguish between the practices of prayer and Scripture study, so throughout this chapter we will look at them as one integrated practice. In fact monastic communities have always made little distinction between the two. As spiritual director Basil Pennington says, "There was just one simple movement of response to a God who speaks not just in the books of the divinely inspired scriptures but in the whole of creation and in the depths of one's own being."[2]

We cannot pray effectively or develop a rich and growing intimacy with God without spending regular time in the Scriptures—reading, meditating, and studying. The apostle Paul tells us, "Whatever is true, whatever is noble, whatever is right, whatever is pure, whatever is lovely, whatever is admirable—if anything is excellent or praiseworthy—think about such things" (Phil. 4:8). It is through entering into the Scriptures that we learn to identify what is true and noble and pure and enable God to renew and transform our minds.

Prayer and Scripture Study—Lifeblood of Our Rhythm

Prayer and Bible study form the lifeblood that pumps energy and purpose into every other part of our lives. They integrate all other rhythms of life. Just as the blood vessels weave their way throughout our bodies, carrying their life-sustaining fluid to every organ and cell, so prayer and Scripture study are meant to intertwine themselves through our spirits, pumping spiritual life and energy into all our activities. Through these practices and their transforming influences, God and our responsibilities as God's kingdom representatives come into focus.

Deep in our hearts most of us know we need to pray and read the Scriptures, and we yearn for the intimacy prayer brings to our relationship with God. Yet for some reason, our spiritual practices are usually the first thing we jettison when we get overbooked and out of control. When we are physically hungry we always find time to eat. When we are exhausted we always manage to carve out time for sleep, but our spiritual hunger often goes unmet. Many of us live with a nagging hunger, a gnawing guilt because we do not pray or read the Scriptures enough.

When the blood supply in our bodies is disrupted, we suffer heart attacks, strokes, blood clots, or other devastating illness. Similarly if our prayers are disrupted or focused in the wrong place, then we become spiritually ill and will never really develop a good healthy life rhythm. Even when we do pray, our prayers sound more like a shopping list for the latest consumer goods than like a conversation with God.

Teach Us to Pray

It is reassuring to know prayer has never been easy nor has it ever come naturally for Jesus' followers. Although the disciples must have grown up with the Jewish rituals of *shema* twice a day and prayer three times a day—morning, afternoon, and sundown—they still needed to learn to pray. Although they had watched Jesus pray in all kinds of situations, seen him connect his prayer life to his public ministry, and watched him use prayer and his relationship to God to mold all he did, they still didn't understand and begged him: "Teach us to pray" (Luke 11:1). Even after Jesus taught them about prayer, they still could not watch with him one hour and fell asleep in the Garden of Gethsemane.

Why do we find it so hard to carve out time for the practices that should be the focal point of life? Why, like the disciples of old, do we still need to come to Jesus with the cry, "Teach us to pray"?

Starving for Prayer

When I worked in the refugee camps in Thailand, we often admitted severely malnourished kids to the hospital. They staggered around on sticklike legs, their sunken eyes peering out at us from sad shriveled faces. Amazingly these kids would sit on their hospital palettes totally indifferent to the bowls of nourishing food around them. When their mothers tried to feed them they often irritably pushed the food away. They were so malnourished that their stomachs had shriveled and food no longer appealed to them. They needed to learn to eat again, and they also needed to learn how to enjoy the food they were eating.

Spiritual malnutrition is just as devastating, and we may not be aware that our spirits have long ago shriveled up. When we are starved for prayer and Scripture study and our spiritual appetites are deadened, prayer loses its appeal. If someone suggests we pray more, it is not surprising that we irritably push the suggestion away—or make excuses for why we can't find time for this essential practice. Yet in the midst of our stress-filled lives we are starving for the essential spiritual nutrients of life and we have no idea how to feed ourselves. We don't realize that we are surrounded by life-giving spiritual food. Like the malnourished kids in the refugee camps, perhaps we need to be force-fed until we reach the point where we are once again able to eat on our own and to relish spiritual food.

There is another reason that we don't pray or read the Scriptures as much as we should. Most of us are afraid that if we pray more and come closer to God, then God will make demands on our lives that will disrupt the comfortable routines we have established around the prevailing culture. As the well-known Catholic spiritual writer Henri Nouwen reminds us, "We want to move closer to God, the source and goal of our existence, but at the same time we realize that the closer we come to God the stronger will be His demand to let go of the many 'safe' structures we have built around ourselves. Prayer is such a radical act because it requires us to criticize our whole way of being in the world, to lay down our old selves and accept our new self, which is Christ. Prayer therefore is the act of dying to all that we consider to be our own and of being born to a new existence which is not of this world."[3] Praying like Jesus did is radical, but it holds the key to eternal life.

How do we move beyond spiritual starvation to eat from the Bread of Life? How do we break down the barriers imposed by the "safe" routines we have built about us and enter into the new life of prayer that Christ so wonderfully modeled? How do we find that healthy rhythm we so desperately need to nourish our spirits?

Finding a Healthy Rhythm

There are three important questions we need to answer to develop a healthy prayer rhythm. First, *why do we pray?*

Second, *how do we pray?* Third, *when do we pray,* or *how does a healthy rhythm look?* Because prayer and Scripture study are our lifeblood and underlie all other rhythms, we will devote a whole chapter to their development. In subsequent chapters we will explore how this rhythm undergirds the pattern of all our other rhythms.

A Journey into Intimacy with God

Teaching malnourished kids to eat was never easy. Often the first step back to health did not begin with the child but with the mother who had given up hope that her child would survive. Teaching a starving child to eat meant first teaching the mother to love her child again. Unless a child knew that he or she was loved, we had little hope of getting him or her to eat.

A healthy rhythm of life must *begin* with the realization that God loves us and wants to dwell in intimate fellowship with us. As spiritual director Basil Pennington says, "God made man to be his intimate friend; that is the message woven through the whole of Scripture. *All* are called to the intimacy of contemplative union with God, not just a chosen few."[4] How amazing! No wonder Richard Foster calls prayer the key to the heart of God. "Real prayer comes not from gritting our teeth but from falling in love."[5] Falling in love with God as an intimate friend is an incredible and life-transforming idea! As in any relationship, intimacy can only develop if we spend lots of time with the one we love. Prayer is not primarily about approaching God with my demands and petitions; it is a *journey into love* and intimacy with God.

Unfortunately the idea of falling in love with God is hard for most of us to grasp. We live in an age that gives little time or place to intimacy. We major in superficial relationships that we discard when we move to a new town or neighborhood. Falling in love conjures up images of sexual lust and passion rather than the enduring intimacy God intends. Yet deep inside we crave love—the unconditional love that only comes from time spent in the presence of God.

Again the psalmists can give us clues to this wonderful, intimate relationship as they pour out their love to God. "I will sing of the Lord's great love forever; with my mouth I will make your faithfulness known through all generations. I will declare that your love stands firm forever, that you established your faithfulness in heaven itself" (Ps. 89:1–2).

I think it was the intimacy of Jesus' relationship with God that the disciples hungered for when they begged him to teach them to pray. They didn't want to know God just as the awesome, majestic God of all creation revealed through the Jewish Torah. More than anything they wanted to know the loving caring compassionate God that the psalmists glimpsed and that Jesus related to so intimately. As theologian James Mulholland tells us, "For Jesus, God was the father we cry out for when we awake in the darkness, in the grip of a nightmare. God was the mother who dries our tears and kisses away our pain when we fall and skin our knee. God was a parent—intimate, loving and committed."[6]

Through prayer we *enter into relationship* with a God who loves us as a parent. Because of God's great love for us, we learn to trust that he not only knows what is best for us but also wants what is best for us.

Cooperation with God

In this place of intimate prayer we glimpse the deepest desire of God's heart—God's longing for a transformed world. Through prayer we become aware that the heart of God's vision is his love for our hurting world. Here too we begin to discern God's will and the ways in which God wants us to reach out to make a difference in that world. The second reason for prayer, therefore, is *to connect us to God's purposes* for our world and for our lives. E. Stanley Jones sums up this aspect of prayer well. He calls prayer "cooperation with God" and goes on to explain what he means: "In prayer you align your desires, your will, your life to God. You and God become agreed on life desires, life purposes, life plans, and you work them out *together* . . . prayer aligns the whole self to the whole Self of God."[7]

"Thy kingdom come. Thy will be done in earth, as it is in heaven" (Matt. 6:10 KJV). Those wonderful words from the Lord's Prayer put God's priorities into focus—birthing a new kingdom in which all creation once again lives in the wholeness and harmony of relationship as God intended. This kingdom is a place in which "[God] will wipe every tear from their eyes. There will be no more death or mourning or crying or pain, for the old order of things has passed away" (Rev. 21:4). This kingdom is a place of mutual care and concern where all are abundantly provided for and all creation is once again submissive to God.

Henri Nouwen reminds us of the importance of this vision: "This is the vision that guides us. This vision makes us share one another's burdens, carry our crosses together, and unite for a better world. This vision takes the despair out of death and the morbidity out of suffering, and opens new horizons. This vision also gives us the energy to manifest its first realization in the midst of the complexities of life. This vision is indeed of a future world but it is no utopia. The future has already begun and is revealed each time strangers are welcomed, the naked are clothed, the sick and prisoners are visited, and oppression is overcome. Through these grateful actions the first glimpses of a new heaven and a new earth can be seen."[8]

The amazing thing is that our creator God invites us to catch hold of this vision and join him in the exciting drama of seeing the world changed—now in partial ways in anticipation of the day when Christ returns and makes all things whole. The importance of buying a new car or accepting a high paying promotion palls into insignificance beside the satisfaction and fulfillment of participating with God in transforming our world.

There are many wonderful internet and print resources available to help us grab hold of God's vision for our world. *Operation World* (www.gmi.org/ow) and Adopt a People global prayer digest (www.global-prayer-digest.org) are excellent resources that can provide a window into this hurting world and its needs. There are also a number of mission organizations that can expose us to the needs of our poorest neighbors. Check out your favorite mission site or look at Tearfund England (www.tearfund.org), one of the most informative sites I have found.

Vessels of God's Love

Of course God *is* concerned about our needs and requests too. But prayer for our lives as expressed in the Lord's Prayer seems to have specific purposes. Jesus tells us to pray for our daily needs and for forgiveness of our sins and for protection from evil (Matt. 6:11–12). Then he reminds us that our own needs and desires are not meant to be the focus of our prayers. "But seek first his kingdom and his righteousness, and all these things will be given to you as well" (Matt. 6:33). The focus of prayer for our lives is meant to be *part* of the journey to intimacy with God. We pray that we will be transformed into "vessels of God's love"[9] so that we will be better equipped to serve God and do his will.

Listen to how Paul expresses this in Romans: "Take your everyday, ordinary life—your sleeping, eating, going-to-work, and walking-around life—and place it before God as an offering. Embracing what God does for you is the best thing you can do for him. Don't become so well adjusted to your culture that you fit into it without thinking. Instead fix your attention on God. You'll be changed from the inside out. Readily recognize what he wants from you, and quickly respond to it. Unlike the culture around you, always dragging you down to its level of immaturity, God brings the best out of you, developing well-formed maturity in you" (Rom. 12:1–2 MESSAGE).

We are all transformed into vessels of love as we lay our lives as an offering before God, as we confess our sins and reach out for God's forgiveness, as we reconcile with those we have hurt and those who have hurt us. In the process we discover that God has created us not to pursue our own selfish ambitions and the aspirations of the consumer culture but to be citizens of God's shalom kingdom. We are created as a community of people God intended to live and work together in harmony and mutual trust, caring for creation and relating personally to a God who walks in intimacy with us.

I come from a dysfunctional family. When I moved to New Zealand as a young doctor, I carried a lot of emotional baggage and pain with me. A friend described me as "a volcano waiting to erupt." And I was. I struggled with anger, loneliness, and intense feelings of rejection. I desperately needed the health and wholeness God promised. I soon discovered, however, that focusing on my own pain and need for healing was not the best path to follow.

The prophet Isaiah sums up the path to my healing. "If you spend yourselves in behalf of the hungry and satisfy the needs of the oppressed, then *your* light will rise in the darkness, and *your* night will become like the noonday. The

Lord will guide you always; he will satisfy your needs in a sun-scorched land and will strengthen your frame. *You will be like a well-watered garden, like a spring whose waters never fail"* (Isa. 58:10–11, emphasis added). Over the last twenty years I have experienced incredible healing in my life, but it has come as I reached out to others and became God's instrument of healing in their lives. Interestingly a growing number of psychiatrists and psychologists encourage their patients to get involved in service projects in their communities because they recognize that it is in giving life away to others that we truly find healing for ourselves.

Finding a Palatable Meal

Surprisingly, malnourished kids are finicky eaters. If we didn't offer them food they really liked then it was hard to get them to eat anything. Of course they didn't all like the same kind of food either. Some liked eggs, some meat. Others needed rice to stimulate their appetites, so we often needed to experiment with different foods until we could offer them a palatable meal.

Similarly prayer comes in many forms and there are no set rules to tell us exactly how to pray or what kind of a diet we should like—but when we do start to pray, like those malnourished kids reaching for a meal, we must make sure that the spiritual food we begin with is something we will really enjoy. I must confess that I am nervous about providing a how-to kit for prospective prayers because I don't want to give the impression that there are correct formulas for prayer. God doesn't answer our prayers because we use the right tools and techniques. God listens and answers because of the deep love he bears toward us.

Learning how to pray and discovering a godly prayer rhythm is an exciting adventure that encourages us to be creative as we enter God's presence in our own unique way. Christians have used certain types of prayer for centuries. Other forms are just being invented, and I suspect that there are still other ways to pray that we haven't discovered. There are, however, a plethora of resources available that can help us develop a framework for our prayer rhythm and journey into intimacy with God.

Balancing Being with Doing

There are two general categories for our prayers: the "being" prayers—those that draw us into God's presence and toward God's love—and the "doing" prayers—those that connect us to God's world and his purposes for us as part of that world. Contemplation, meditation, and sacramental prayer are examples of "being" prayers. Intercession, healing prayer, and blessing prayers are examples of "doing" prayers.

Some of us grow up in traditions that emphasize the doing side. We are eager to change the world and convert our fellow travelers. Any suggestion that we might pause to take stock of our lives we dismiss as laziness or half-heartedness. Others of us emphasize being. We like to meditate and ponder on the presence of God. We like to cultivate the inward journey and are more concerned about what goes on in the deep recesses of our hearts than with what is happening in the world.

Both of these conditions create unhealthy rhythms. If we stick to only one form of prayer, we are like a person who eats only one kind of food. Our diet is boring and terribly unhealthy, and we soon get sick of it. Once we are praying regularly it is important to add other "food"—those types of prayer that may seem less palatable but that provide the vitamins and minerals necessary for a healthy well-balanced prayer life. We need both the being and the doing prayers. If we place too much emphasis on doing, we tend to think that God wants us to be busy every moment and we are prone to overextend and overcommit ourselves. If we emphasize the being side, we can easily disengage from our hurting world.

Initially what attracts us to prayer depends on our faith traditions, cultural heritage, life experiences, and personalities. The Celtic monks often prayed for hours, standing up to their necks in icy streams—not something that has the least appeal for me. My early experience of prayer focused mainly on intercession for friends, family, and the world around me. It was very much a doing form of prayer with little time for quiet reflection and contemplation. Now I like to pray sitting quietly in my room or out in the garden or during a walk around the lake. Though doing is important, just being in the presence of God is even more important and should be a prelude to activity-generating prayers like intercession and healing.

Enjoying God's Feast

A cross made from Post It notes, a wall of "prayer graffiti," candles burning to offer prayers for unsaved friends are but a few of the rich and innovative expressions of prayer one encounters when exploring the 24-7 Prayer website. This incredible network has become a worldwide movement, linking hundreds of nonstop prayer meetings via the web to form a unique chain of prayer that literally spans the globe. Amazingly it all started by accident when a bunch of young people in England got the crazy idea of trying to pray nonstop for a month. "God turned up and they couldn't stop till Christmas!" Since then the 24-7 prayer movement has spread around the world, igniting young people with the dream "to turn the tide of youth culture back to Jesus."[10]

One of the keys to the success of the 24-7 prayer network has been the establishment of prayer rooms, specific locations in which people gather to pray twenty-four hours a day. These rooms enable young people to use their creativity and imagination as they pray. Because many of the participants are visually oriented, they often pray nonverbally by posting artwork, poetry, and graffiti on the walls. Some draw or paint pictures. Others write Scripture verses, poetry, or prayers on big sheets of paper. Others prefer to light candles or listen to music while they pray out loud to God. Prayer rooms have been established in weird and wonderful locations like a skate park in Switzerland, a bus in the slums of Delhi, and a police station in London as well as more conventional places like churches, student dorm rooms, and chapels. As they gather in these rooms, young people everywhere are learning the power of prayer as they share each other's burdens, minister to one another, and celebrate God's answers.[11]

Our God is a God of infinite variety, so it isn't surprising that this is reflected in the myriad of ways that are available for us to pray. One way to fire your imagination is by visiting some web sites on prayer like the 24-7 prayer network or the Taize community in France (www.taize.fr). Also try Scripture Union (www.scriptureunion.org.uk) and the Guidepost site (www.dailyguidepost.com). Other sites cater to almost every imaginable group from kids to educators to housewives and business people. So get on-line and check them out. You might find something you can use as a framework for your own prayer rhythm.

Another way to learn how to pray is to explore the various prayer traditions—from contemplative prayer and meditation to intercessory and sacramental prayer. Experiment a little and work on a discipline that feels comfortable. One creative possibility that connects prayer to everyday routines is to identify landmarks as you walk or drive to work or school.

Associate each landmark with a particular person, church, or ministry and pray for them each time you see this landmark. This is a helpful way to restore the rhythm of prayer to our busy lives.

How do you want to begin your journey into intimacy with God? Do you like to pray in private, or would you prefer to get together with a group of friends to start on this most important adventure? Do you like spontaneous prayers, or are you more attracted to liturgical expressions of prayer? Choose a place to start, and block out five minutes for prayer. What small goals could you set to reflect your beginner status? How could you add new ideas and possibilities as you accomplish your beginning goals?

Exploring the Options

One of my favorite prayer resources is Richard Foster's book *Prayer: Finding the Heart's True Home*. In it he explores prayer in its many forms. He shows how different types of prayer can move us upward toward intimacy with God, inward toward personal transformation, and outward toward ministry and service for others. Foster reminds us not to be discouraged by our lack of prayer because "even in our prayerlessness we can hunger for God." He goes on to add: "In time the desire will lead to practice, and practice will increase the desire."[12] Just as malnourished children's hunger grows as they begin to eat, so our hunger for prayer grows as we practice it.

Foster suggests that the best place to start our prayer life is with what he calls "simple prayer," a form of prayer in which we just talk to God about the mundane daily stuff of our lives, sharing our hurts and our anger, our sorrows and disillusionments, our joys and our accomplishments. "God listens in compassion and love, just like we do when our children come to us. He delights in our presence. When we do this, we will discover something of inestimable value. We will discover that by praying we learn to pray."[13]

Learning to Listen

If all we ever do in our prayers is talk to God and recite prayers of blessing, we will never really develop the intimacy that we crave and that God longs for. Intimacy does not develop from a one-sided monologue. Christian statesman Oswald Chambers tells us, "The destiny of my spiritual life is such identification with Jesus that I always hear God, and I know that God always hears me." Eventually we must learn to sit in quiet and listen to God cultivating what Chambers calls "the devotion of hearing."[14] As spiritual director Jan Johnson explains in her book *When the Soul Listens,* "Those with hearing ears who accept what God says are the ones who become partners with him in the work of his kingdom."[15]

Sitting quietly, listening to God is not easy for those of us who live in a world of constant noise and incessant activity, yet it is essential if we are serious about connecting our lives to God. Jesus constantly withdrew into quiet places to pray. We too may need to schedule times to withdraw into a quiet place for "dates" with God in our daily and weekly schedule planning. "When we make intentional time for solitude, that is, when we put ourselves in a secluded, lonely, remote habitation, one absent of stir, a strange thing occurs. We set our face to no other distractions but the face of God. We look to him. As we do, our spiritual character becomes solid: The interior is completely filled up and made strong, firm and substantial. We develop a solidarity with God, the Triune Spirit, becoming united with his heart, perspective and being."[16] What a beautiful thought—to develop solidarity with the Triune God. In that place of solidarity with God all other forms of prayer find their purpose and their focus. Prayers of adoration and worship bubble up from within, pain for God's broken world overflows in intercessions for others, and prayers for our own healing and wholeness radiate from a desire to break down the barriers that isolate us from God.

Blending the Old and the New

In the last few years Christians of many traditions have shown a resurgence of interest in one creative form of prayer called the labyrinth. It can help us find solitude in the midst of our noisy world. In the cathedrals of medieval Europe mazelike pathways were often marked out on the floors. As a group of townsfolk moved along the path toward the center of the labyrinth, their journey symbolized an inner movement toward Christ. Youth for Christ London director Jonny Baker has reworked the labyrinth in ways that appeal to a growing number of young people around the world. "Labyrinth blends ancient and contemporary in an exciting way," he explains in an article in *Youthwork*. "Labyrinth reshapes what was a 12th century ritual, blending tradition with technology and creating a multi-sensory experience which includes visuals, rituals, meditations, sounds, art, media and symbolic activity."[17]

Participants entering the labyrinth are given a portable CD player with specially prepared meditations that guide them through eleven stations as they walk the maze. Walking toward the center through each station, participants focus on the inward journey of faith and their need to let go of hurts and distractions. The center itself provides a "Holy Space" whose meditation encourages partakers to "commune with God and receive from God." Then the outward journey focuses on outward expressions of faith. The "noise" station invites participants to light an electronic candle on a laptop for someone they know. The "planet" station flashes onscreen images of earth from space as a backdrop to a meditation on escaping one's boundaries. Participants walk the labyrinth alone, enjoying the solitude and reflecting on their understanding of faith.

There is also an on-line labyrinth at www.labyrinth.org.uk where people can enjoy the experience at home. "One aspect of the consumer culture that we live in is that people want experiences to weave meaning into their lives," says Jonny Baker.[18] The labyrinth is certainly one spiritual expression that can help accomplish this for people of all ages.

Integrating Word and Prayer

To help them remain consistent in their pursuit of holiness, ancient monastic Christians used another enriching spiritual practice, which you may want to explore. It is *lectio divina*, loosely translated "divine reading," a unified discipline with four connected stages, which Clifford Bajema explains in his booklet *At One with Jesus*.[19] *Lectio divina* is designed to move the Word of God off the page and into our hearts so that it becomes living and active in our lives. It begins with reading the Scripture *(lectio)*. This is more than a cursory reading of the text. It may mean reading the Scripture over and over in an atmosphere of prayer for illumination. Or it can involve studying dictionaries and commentaries to understand the intent of the author. Sometimes it sends us to consult spiritual directors to gain understanding. It challenges us to memorize the Scriptures until they resonate in our spirits.

The second step is meditation *(meditatio)*. "Meditation allows us to go beyond information to inspiration, beyond observation to evaluation, beyond memorization to imagination. . . . As Brother Lawrence has said, in meditation we exercise our godliness. We practice the presence of God."[20] Richard Foster explains, "Christian meditation leads us to the inner wholeness necessary to give ourselves to God freely, and to the spiritual perception necessary to attack social evils."[21]

The third step is prayer *(oratio)* literally conversing with God about the Scripture. We listen to God, gaining direction, guidance, and comfort. Sometimes we are convicted of sin and seek forgiveness. Through this kind of prayer our lives are illuminated and transformed.

The last step is contemplation *(contemplatio)*. "In contemplation, worshipers become a 'living sacrifice.' . . . God becomes fixed in our memory, in our actions, and in our character. . . . Individually and communally we become Jesus' hands, eyes, feet and heart."[22] To find our true identity as Jesus' hands, eyes, and feet is the longing within the heart of God for all followers of Christ. "For we are God's workmanship, created in Christ Jesus to do good works, which God prepared in advance for us to do" (Eph. 2:10). What a wonderful thought! How wonderful to see that fulfilled as we step into the rhythm of life God intends for us.

Listen to the Beat—Prescription for Life

Have you ever wondered what would have happened to the disciples if they had stayed awake with Jesus in the Garden of Gethsemane? Would they have realized that Jesus' death and betrayal was not defeat but the focal point of all human history? Would they have been able to trust that God was in control of the horrific events enacted in front of their eyes on that first Good Friday? Would they have recognized Jesus sooner after his resurrection?

What about our lives? God still comes to us, wanting to teach us to pray and inviting us to reach out for the intimacy that comes from placing prayer at the center of all we do. Will you accept this invitation and allow prayer to become the integrating rhythm, the lifeblood that pumps energy and purpose through all you are and do?

1. *Spend some time reflecting on what it means to "fall in love with God." Write a love letter to God that expresses your thoughts and feelings.*
2. *In what ways do you feel called to be a "vessel of God's love" to your family, friends, and the world? How would you need to shape your prayer life in order to be better equipped for this task?*
3. *What types of prayer most appeal to you? How could you change your schedule to set aside five minutes each day to make prayer an integral part of your life rhythm?*

6

RHYTHM FOR THE DAY

*W*hen was the last time your class saw how 'HOT' God's Word is?" proclaims the sales blurb for a new inflammatory Bible. "Open this authentic-looking 'Bible' and begin to share the scripture for the day as real flames are seen coming from your 'Bible.' This full size book comes with a battery operated ignition system. All you supply are the batteries, lighter fluid and composure."[1] Imagine how this purchase could warm up your Bible study group!

Balancing Your Prayer Life

How does a healthy daily spiritual rhythm look, and do we really need gimmicks like a flaming Bible to motivate us?

Perhaps we can learn a lesson from Carolus Linnaeus, an eighteenth-century Swedish botanist who was so intrigued by the daily rhythms he observed in plants that he grew a garden that could tell time. Every hour from morning to evening, a different flower in his garden opened or closed its blossoms.[2] Sounds incredible doesn't it? Can you imagine the time and effort he must have expended on that garden before it bloomed? I suspect it took years for him to cultivate all the plants to flower exactly as planned.

Many of us want to develop a prayer life that is constantly blooming like Carolus's garden. We crave spiritual practices that enliven every hour and feel guilty because we do not practice the prayer "without ceasing" we read about in 1 Thessalonians 5:17. Most of us find it difficult to set aside more than a few minutes a day for prayer.

Fortunately learning to pray as Jesus prayed does not mean gorging on forty days of prayer and fasting out in the wilderness—nor does it mean starting with a spiritual routine that is constantly in bloom. Again Richard Foster provides us with insights. "If prayer is not a fixed habit with you, instead of starting with twelve hours of prayer-filled dialogue, single out a few moments and put all your energy into them. When you have had enough, tell God simply, 'I must rest; I have no strength to be with you all the time.' This by the way is perfectly true, and God knows that you are still not capable of bearing his company continuously. Besides, even the most spiritually advanced—perhaps *especially* the most spiritually advanced—need frequent times of laughter and play and good fun."[3]

So where do we start? At a creativity seminar my husband and I held in Winnipeg, Manitoba, a couple years ago, one of the participants came up with the following anagram as a suggestion for a healthy spiritual pattern to govern our lives—divert daily, withdraw weekly, maintain monthly, and abandon annually. And she is right. There are spiritual practices that should shape our days, others that should focus our weeks, and others that provide direction and guidance to our monthly and yearly schedules. In this chapter we will examine the rituals and routines that can shape our daily schedules, and in subsequent chapters will take a closer look at the rhythms that can shape our weeks and years.

Starting in the Right Place

In *Receiving the Day: Christian Practices for Opening the Gift of Time,* Dorothy Bass suggests that the place to start as we develop our daily rhythm of prayer is not in the morning but when we go to bed at night. She reminds us that for the Hebrews, and in the biblical story, a day begins at dusk not at dawn. When we view time in this way, it changes our perceptions. Each day begins with God's activity rather than our own productivity. "The first part of the day passes in darkness, then, but not in inactivity. God is out growing the crops even before the farmer is up and knitting together the wound before the clinic opens. When farmer and physician awake, they will join in, contributing mightily, but only because God came first. Likewise, God has been working on and in them, body and mind, while they slept; yesterday's bruises and slights have begun to heal. . . . Morning becomes a time to join in the labors that have already begun without us, and evening a time to let others—and Another—take over."[4]

I love this concept! Evening—a beginning—a time to start afresh, to relinquish all our frustrations and pressures to God so that as we sleep he can begin the healing process in our bodies and minds. More than that it is a time to reflect on where we have met God during the day and evaluate how we have accomplished God's kingdom purposes in our activities. Doing so not only raises our awareness of God's constant presence with us but also instills in us gratitude and expectation. God has been present today, and will also be tomorrow.

This idea is particularly helpful for busy people who leave home early to get to work. Trying to squeeze daily devotions into an already over-crowded morning just adds one more pressure to our overbooked schedules. What a relief—and a relaxation—to start our prayer rhythm at bedtime. To know that God is at work long before we get up and get going in the morning takes the burden of the day's accomplishments from *our* shoulders and places it fairly and squarely on *God's* instead. We can sit back and relax. God is in control, and we don't need to fill every minute with busy activity to accomplish God's kingdom purposes.

In *Sleeping with Bread: Holding What Gives You Life,* Dennis and Sheila Linn share how they light a candle each evening to focus on God's loving presence. They sit quietly for about five minutes, and then ask each other two questions: "For what moment today am I most grateful?" and "For what moment today am I least grateful?" Reflecting on these questions, they point out, connects us to God's presence directing and guiding us through every moment of the day. It helps us realize how God works through the seemingly insignificant and ordinary events of our days. "Insignificant moments when looked at each day become significant because they form a pattern that often points the way to how God wants to give us more life."[5]

How could you reinvent your bedtime rituals to include a few minutes of this kind of reflective prayer? What would assist you to focus on God's purposes for your day's activities and enable you to release all your frustrations and stresses to God? The thoughts we end the day with often go with us into our unconscious sleeping state. What difference would it make if those last thoughts were gratitude and thankfulness toward God?

Don't Forget the Morning Boost

An old story tells of a godly monk who was training young men to become priests. He asked the novitiates a riddle. "How do you know when the darkness is dispelled and the dawn has come?"

The young students puzzled over the riddle for hours. "Is it when we can distinguish a palm from a pomegranate?" one of them asked.

The monk shook his head.

"Is it when we can tell the difference between a dog and a goat?" asked another.

"No," said the old monk.

The students were silent.

Finally, the wise old man answered his own riddle. "We know that the darkness is dispelled and the dawn has come," he told them, "when we can see in the countenance of another the face of Christ."

What is the first thought you concentrate on when you get up in the morning? It may shape the rest of your day.

For most of us a morning prayer boost is just as necessary for our spiritual lives as breakfast is for our physical bodies—and many nutritionists tell us that breakfast is the most important meal of the day. This is the time that we (or at least most of us) begin our work. We are most easily distracted from our relationship with God and his kingdom purposes as the pressures and stresses of the day overtake us. Block out five minutes for prayer each morning—not prayer for your needs or the needs of others, but prayer that helps you focus on your love relationship with God and on his purposes for your life. Just as we need to take God's presence with us into our unconscious sleep, so we need to take his presence into the busyness of our days. When we do, it impacts the way we view ourselves and those around us.

I suggest you start by reciting a line or two of Scripture or a simple prayer you have memorized. If you have more time, a devotional book is a good investment. Of course there are more devotionals available than there are translations of the Bible! One enduring classic is *My Utmost for His Highest* by Oswald Chambers. Another challenging book is *Near to the Heart of God: Daily Readings from the Spiritual Classics* by Bernard Bangley.

If you need something lighter or are overcommitted, try *Pace Yourself: Daily Devotions for Those Who Do Too Much* by Ric Engram. A helpful little devotional book that explores some of the compulsions that govern our lives, *Pace Yourself* provides meditations to assist in breaking the cycles that contribute to these destructive patterns. When our minds are undisciplined in the art of prayer and even more so when our commitments tug us in a hundred directions at once, it is hard to concentrate without assistance. Devotional books are a tremendous boost.

I love to sit in our breakfast room for my morning prayer time, looking out on the changing seasons and patterns of the days. Sometimes the Olympic Mountains, rising snow covered and majestic in the distance, catch my attention and draw me into the awesome majesty of God. At other times the fragrance of the blossoming lilac tree outside the window reminds me that incense is "the prayers of the saints" (Rev. 5:8) in God's sight.

Several times a week I read my mission statement aloud: "To be a voice for those who have no voice and bring glimpses of God's shalom kingdom into peoples' lives."[6] My mission statement helps me focus my day intentionally on God's purposes rather than my own self-centered ambitions. Then I reflect on the day's schedule and think about how I will live out that mission statement. I end with a short prayer, committing all my activities into God's hands. Particularly when I am stressed, overwhelmed, and out of control, I find that this act of commitment helps relieve some of the pressure. It also often enables me to be more realistic about what I should and should not be involved in. Amazingly though I do less, I seem to accomplish more—at least more of the things that really matter.

My friend John, who commutes an hour to work each day, has found a simple solution for his morning prayer time. He rides the bus to work rather than driving his car. "It is just as fast and much cheaper as I don't need to find a place to park," he said. "We zip along in the carpool lane bypassing much of the other traffic. It's far less stressful and I have ample time for prayer and Bible study along the way."

David has discovered another creative approach to free up time in the morning. He arrives at work fifteen minutes earlier than he used to and sits in his car to pray and read his Bible before going to the office. On the way home he often stops at a viewpoint about a mile from his house. "I love to be able to decompress after the work day," he said. "I can give all the frustrations of the day to God, and then when I get home I am fully present to my wife and kids."

I think that one of Jesus' regular questions to God must have been, "Okay, where do I go today, and what am I supposed to do with my time?" Of course he didn't have a day planner or palm pilot, but if he did I can imagine him pulling out his schedule each morning and praying over each meeting and appointment before he started the day.

Prayer Works Better than Prozac

A recent sign outside a pharmacy in Texas read, "Generic Prozac now available; in God we trust." Obviously the pharmacy had rather divided loyalties! In the long run if we really want to learn to trust in God rather than in the power of Prozac, prayer needs to become more than a five-minute devotional to lubricate our day. As in Jesus' life, it must become part of the very framework that holds our days and activities together. Esther de Waal says, "Life must flow into prayer, each day is to be broken up by times of prayer, praying and living are inseparable."[7]

Of course believing that we need this kind of prayer life is one thing. Putting it into action is another. To be honest, the busier I get the *less* time I take for prayer and the more inclined I am to make hasty decisions about what to do with my time and energy. When I am stressed out and overwhelmed, or if I am depressed and down in the dumps, there is nothing harder for me than to take a few minutes to pray. Instead, I want to escape into a sci-fi novel or go to the mall. Busyness becomes a shortcut straight into the temptations of our consumer culture.

Spiritual Breathing—Rhythm for the Road

Sara Wenger Shenk has some helpful insights here. "Learning how to cultivate the presence of God throughout our daily activities can be a revolutionary discovery. Prayer doesn't need to be a formal, lengthy exercise that one only gets around to now and then. Instead, prayer can be like breathing, like continually feeling loved by God. With a little discipline we can learn to offer our activities, small and large, to God, doing what we would normally do, but doing it for the love of God. As we do for God's sake what we normally do for ourselves, each deed, no matter how mundane, can become an act of worship. When prayer accompanies all that we do, our whole life becomes an offering of prayer."[8]

In chapter 3 we looked at some of the ways we can incorporate short prayers and informal blessings into our daily activities, but there are many other creative ways in which this can be achieved. The goal is to develop a spiritual rhythm that intertwines throughout the day, providing a pulse for all we do.

One suggestion is to develop "prayer breaks" throughout the day, just as we would take coffee or tea breaks. In fact, coffee and tea breaks can be a good time to institute these practices. Pause for a minute or two and say a short prayer, refocusing your life on God and his purposes. If you are sitting in front of your computer, you may like to go to an online devotional site. If you are musically inclined, you might like to sing a song that conveys something of your sense of purpose. You could recite a prayer or a Scripture that you heard in church on Sunday. The advantage of this is that it connects your spiritual breaks back to your church community and Sunday worship. Doing so enriches both your work life and your Sunday worship.

There are some excellent resources to assist you in this type of prayer break. David Adam's little book, *The Rhythm of Life,* has short prayer services for morning, noon, evening, and night designed "to help people to rejoice constantly in the presence of the living God."[9] Each day of the week has a different theme. I have used his themes as a template for my devotions, as I talked about in chapter 4, and found them to be helpful. Using some of the themes Adam suggests and substituting a few of my own, I have developed short morning prayers and devotional rituals that help me deliberately connect my daily life to my faith.

David Adam suggests that we memorize these prayers and say them aloud—what he calls "recital theology." "By reciting aloud, we use our eyes, mouth and ears as well as our minds. Reading aloud produces a physical vibration that affects not only our ears but our heart and our minds also so that when we hear the words in a different context an echoing chord is struck in our being, setting off a whole melody of associations. Once we have words in our heart, a phrase, or even a single word, can pluck at our heartstrings and cause us to react."[10] And that is part of what prayer without ceasing is about—responding to the pluck at our heartstrings, which the association of words, images or sounds produces for us.

Another place to start finding your spiritual rhythm may be by using short prayers in conjunction with everyday events, as suggested in chapter 3. This is a great place to get creative—write your own prayers to connect these events to your faith. Or you might like to take photos or draw pictures or write music that can bring a sense of the awe-inspiring presence of God into these everyday events. Several years ago I developed my own prayers for different daily events. Here is one that I have found helpful for beginning a busy workday. It is fashioned on some of the ancient Celtic prayers that I have come to love. It may not win any prizes for poetic expression, but it helps me to enter the day with a sense that the Triune God goes with me in everything I do.

> As we journey forth this day, Almighty God protect we
> pray.
> Be our shield, our strength our guide in city office or as we
> ride.
> Keep us Savior strong and true, as we seek to follow you.
> Through the crowded streets of life, Spirit keep us from all
> strife.
> Keep our vision on the Three, Father, Son and Spirit,
> Blessed Trinity.

Another helpful suggestion Father Fitzgerald offers in his book *Blessings for the Fast Paced and Cyberspaced* for people who spend a lot of time on the computer is to form a prayer partnership with others who are constantly online. Each partner then uses the booting up moment at the beginning of the day as a time to pause for a short, shared prayer ritual.

> Before I travel on the information highway,
> In this moment of waiting
> I pause to remember _____ in prayer.
> Bless their (his/her) booting.
> Bless their (his/her) working.
> Bless their (his/her) journeys.
> As we enter cyberspace,
> May we hold each other in our heart space.[11]

Karen Cho, a Korean student at Regent College in Vancouver, found that singing Scripture songs while she studied revolutionized her day. Now she sometimes sings and studies for hours on end.

Reviving an Ancient Rhythm

David Robinson, a Presbyterian pastor, started making annual retreats to Benedictine monasteries a number of years ago and through that experience has made prayer a more regular part of his day and his family's rituals. "According to Benedict, seven times a day is not too often for families to pray to God," Robinson says in *The Family Cloister.* He suggests we can adapt this process by setting aside seven times during the day for short prayers. He has done an excellent job of connecting these times to daily routines:

- In the morning praise God for the new day and read a psalm.
- While bathing confess your sins and ask God to cleanse your heart and mind.

- Say grace before breakfast.
- Pause during morning break and breathe in God's goodness.
- Say a prayer at lunchtime.
- Hold hands around the dinner table to receive God's grace at night.
- At bedtime, kneel together, say the Lord's Prayer, and pray God's blessing for others.[12]

Evidently it was out of this ritual of regular prayers throughout the day that clocks were invented by monks who wanted to ensure they stopped at the right time of the day and night to pray. How ironic that an instrument designed to help us focus our faith observances has instead become the controller of our lives—usually keeping us away from things of faith rather than drawing us toward them.

Unfortunately, sometimes human attempts to overcome a problem are superficial and more embarrassing than the problem itself. We now have watches with Bible verses and portraits of Jesus. You can even buy a Hallelujah clock embellished with a portrait of Jesus, surrounded by "memorable events from his life." It plays the "Hallelujah Chorus" from Handel's *Messiah* every hour on the hour. As it does so, the clock's six petals spring into view, each showing an angel in a glitzy pose.[13]

In all seriousness, creativity in developing prayer rituals tailored to our own schedules and personality types can be good. For those with long commutes, travel time might provide a chance to refocus. Before lunch and dinner and again at bedtime, you might recite a simple prayer that helps you refocus on God's shalom purposes. At a recent seminar one participant, Helen, jumped at this suggestion. "And no one would need to know I was doing it either," she confided. "I could just pretend I was finishing off my work before lunch."

If you work at night or on a rotating shift, you may like to develop a routine that has a more flexible pattern.

If you spend a lot of time online, you can use an almost endless list of prayer devotionals. Using the Google search engine, I recently searched for "prayer devotionals" and got almost a million responses. My favorite response said, "Morning and evening prayer has moved. Please click the link to continue." That expressed my sentiments exactly. Morning and evening prayer has moved; for most of us it has moved right out of our lives.

All joking aside there are some excellent resources available on the internet. Sacred Space, the prayer site run by the Irish Jesuits (www.jesuit.ie/prayer), is a wonderful site that invites you, as you sit at your computer, to spend ten minutes praying with the help of on-screen guidance and Scripture chosen specially every day. There are also a number of sites that are designed to help busy people find a way to participate in morning and evening prayer. The Mission of St. Clare runs one of the best of these (www.missionstclare.com). Its goal is "to establish tiny meditation spaces within office complexes and shopping areas." Using *The Book of Common Prayer*, it provides online daily offices complete with readings and psalms for each day and even a bit of music. How enriching such an experience can be as we pause during the day bringing a sense of the sacred into the most secular of environments.

One of the things I love about the readings from *The Book of Common Prayer* is that they integrate Old and New Testament passages around a common theme. An incredible amount of work must have gone into developing this kind of integration. My Bible study comes to life as I understand the rich connection between the Old and New Testament stories. For those who spend much time writing and responding to e-mail, there are other sites that will e-mail you a daily devotional that could provide a welcome spiritual break in the midst of your work.

When Tom visited Mother Teresa's Sisters of Charity in Calcutta, India, he discovered that they have a beautiful rhythm of daily life, which connects them to the sacred in the midst of their often painful ministry to the poor and destitute. They begin the day with a eucharistic service, taking into themselves the body and the blood of Christ and visualizing the presence of Christ flowing into them. Then as they go out among the poor and destitute on the streets of Calcutta, they see themselves as giving out the love and compassion of Christ from this reservoir. At the same time, they recognize Christ in the pain and suffering of their patients and absorb that into themselves. Finally, at the end of the day they give the pain and suffering back to Christ at another eucharistic service.

When we live in the daily awareness of God's presence, our minds, bodies, and spirits are enriched and renewed. There are so many ways we can connect to the sacred presence. All it takes is a little time, a little discipline, and a lot of perseverance.

Kids Grow Better with Prayer

There are many creative ways to introduce a daily prayer and Scripture rhythm into the lives of our children too. When my friend Patty picks up her kids, Jake and Dustin, from school in the afternoon, she asks them, "What was the best thing about the day, and what was the worst?" At first it took them a while to respond, but now they jump in the car eager to share and to pray about the day's happenings.

Sometimes daily prayer may be a little difficult with the stress of getting kids off to school in the morning, but at least one morning a week should be set aside for family prayers.

David and Karen introduced a family breakfast on Saturday mornings. The family reads a short devotional together and then has a time of prayer. As the children grew older they took increasing responsibility for the family ritual, which gradually became a daily occurrence. The kids feel the day hasn't really started until they've prayed together. "Even if it is just as we rush out the door, it still gives an incredible sense of security to all of us," Karen said. "A prayer of blessing before each child leaves for school and a prayer of thanksgiving as they return are beautiful ways to connect them to the sense that God goes with them as they leave the house and guides them through all the activities of the day."

Jesus put his hands on children and blessed them when people brought them to him (Mark 10:13). In the same way we can bless and empower our children as they go out each day into the hectic world. Saying grace at meals, praying with the kids, and reading Bible or missionary stories before they go to sleep are all ways to impart a sense of the spiritual into the mundane. At night asking the question "Where did you meet God today?" and talking about the frustrations and concerns children have experienced help them connect their everyday activities to God and his purposes for them.

Prayer with a Missionary Focus

Tim and Helen have a map on the wall with the location of all the church missionaries marked on it. Their kids, Christopher and Melanie, regularly correspond with the missionaries by e-mail and once a week give the rest of the family an update. Then they lead a time of prayer for their far-flung network of friends. It has not only helped them develop their own prayer disciplines but also given them a wonderful feeling of connection to the worldwide body of Christ.

As kids enter the teenage years, these family prayer disciplines may need to be rethought. Teenagers want to establish their own identities and often need to break away from their families to do this. However, they also struggle with how to know God's will, so they can be very receptive to other spiritual advisors. Encouraging prayer with friends or youth groups, Big Sister or Big Brother relationships, and Adopt a Grandparent programs all help provide the spiritual focus that is so necessary during this important formative time. Of course prayer resources already mentioned such as the 24-7 prayer network and the labyrinth can be attractive prayer routines for young people. Interestingly the 24-7 prayer movement has discovered that young people are more likely to sign up for prayer at 3 A.M. than they are at 7 P.M. The experience of something that is radical or extreme may appeal to them more than the mundane and the ordinary.

Prayer Goes Better in Groups

Teenagers are not the only ones who need the wider Christian community to strengthen their prayer times. We are all enriched by group prayer and Bible study. For singles and solo parents in particular, a weekly lunch or breakfast with a small group of friends to fellowship, pray, and read Scripture may be an important discipline that not only connects you to each other but also to God and his purposes for you and the world around you. Tom and I belong to a small group of seven people who get together once a month. We start with a meal and some good fellowship, then sit down for some more serious spiritual input. Often we ask each other, "When did you feel closest to God this last week?" or, "When did you feel farthest from God?" Both of these questions provide a good basis for spiritual discussion. We always end with a time of prayer for personal needs or global concerns.

Are We Caught in the Time Bind?

The prayer practices we propose to help us live more satisfying and less pressurized lives take time, time we feel we can ill afford in our already overstretched lives. This brings us to an examination of the commitments we *do* make. That forces us to ask ourselves two questions: "What do I need to add? What do I need to take away from my schedule?"

What activities in your schedule could you sacrifice to make time each day for prayer? Do you spend too much time in front of the TV or shopping or on the Internet or at sporting events? Are your kids too involved in soccer or basketball or ballet?

The tenacity with which we hold onto the controlling schedules and idols of the consumer culture reveals how radically different God intended our daily rhythms to be. The flickering images of the TV screen distract our attention for hours without our even realizing how much time we are wasting. The lure of the internet provides twenty-four-hour-a-day access to the consumer marketplace and entertainment industry. Peer pressure calling for involvement in children's sports and other extracurricular activities constantly competes with God's design for our time.

When Stuart, a vice president in a major U.S. corporation, decided he needed to spend an hour in prayer and Bible study each morning, he realized he had to make significant changes in his schedule. First, he had to go to bed earlier. To get up at 5:30 A.M. he needed to be in bed by 10 P.M. at the latest. That meant less TV and fewer evenings out. "At first it seemed like a real sacrifice," he said. "But after a while I realized how much more relaxed I was. I was sleeping better and my aches and pains had disappeared. And best of all I found myself becoming more and more excited as I not only spent more time with God but also watched God answer my prayers. Now I find myself wanting to pray more during the day too, and I am actually scheduling time on my palm pilot for prayer breaks. I find everything I do works so much better when I have this kind of commitment."

Listen to the Beat—Check Your Daily Rhythm

A rhythm of prayer that entwines throughout the day truly is the heartbeat of our Christian life. Incorporating it into our days may come at great cost to other commitments, but it also brings a wonderful sense of freedom and joy. Knowing that each day is committed to God and his purposes renews our vision of time and life. It frees us to say no to the unessential and opens our hearts to the unexpected. Let's grab hold of God's gift of time and learn to walk to a different beat. Boldly step out on God's pathway and join those faithful people who are already thinking and living this new way.

1. *Over the next week set aside five to ten minutes for prayer and Scripture reading each day. Experiment with different formats and different times during the day. How could you reinvent your daily schedule to incorporate short breaks for prayer and Scripture study on a regular basis? What would be a creative way for you to remind yourself of this discipline?*
2. *Sit down with your family and discuss the need for a weekly time of prayer. What activities in your schedule and your family's schedule would you need to change to make time each week to pray? What would you all need to do to realistically establish a weekly time for family prayers and Scripture study?*

7

THE SABBATH REST

*I*n her book *Jewish Days: A Book of Jewish Life and Culture,* Francine Klagsbrun introduces us to the wonder of the Sabbath day. She calls its inauguration a miracle because evidently no such day existed until it appeared in the Hebrew Bible—and it is the one rhythm that has no counterpart in the natural world.

She reflects on her father's impressions of the Sabbath, or *Shabbat* as it is called in Hebrew. "'When I was a young man, an immigrant from Russia,' he would say, 'the United States had no labour laws regulating working conditions. People worked long hours, seven days a week, without rest. But imagine, more than three thousand years ago the Bible commanded that all work stop for an entire day every single week, and not only for the ancient Israelites but for all who lived among them, including slaves. And not only for people, but for animals as well. What a revolutionary practice that was. What a miracle!'"[1] Klagsbrun goes on to explain, "The rhythm of the Jewish calendar flows around this day of rest and reflection. In every week of every month of every year, the Sabbath arrives to re-create that moment after Creation when God rested and the entire cosmos was in peace and harmony. Shabbat may be a miracle, as my father taught me. It is also a unique gift only fully appreciated when used."[2]

The celebration of Sabbath, the day of rest, is one of the most beautiful rituals in Jewish culture. The day begins at dusk on Friday with joyous services at the synagogue to welcome its arrival. Even before that the focus for Jewish people has turned to preparation for this day that is, for many, the culmination of the week, the day that sets the purpose for every other day. The ritual greeting, *"Shabbat Shalom,"* bridges the close of the workweek and the beginning of the Sabbath celebrations.

Sabbath is a family event. In each home, the woman of the house lights two candles to symbolize the first act of creation, the separation of light from darkness, and a canopy of peace and repose descends as the family sings a Sabbath hymn. Then there is a time of blessing. First, parents bless their children as an act of love and concern, and then, they pay tribute to each other by singing from the Book of Proverbs. The *kiddush,* recited over a brimming cup of wine, sanctifies the Sabbath before dinner begins.[3]

Sabbath Rest Boosts Better than Vitamins

Not only do we need to reconnect to the holiness of time and God's sacred intended rhythms for us in our day-to-day activities but also we need him to govern our week and our year. God intends to reign over all that we do. There is no better place to find this connection to God's rhythm than in the rediscovery of the Sabbath principle and our God-ordained need for a regular day of rest and spiritual refreshment.

"The human soul needs time to digest, absorb and comprehend emotions and experience," wrote Wayne Muller, author of *Sabbath: Restoring the Sacred Rhythm of Rest.* "Regardless of the external pressure of coercion, the soul cannot be rushed. We must metabolize events and feelings in order to fully apprehend and understand our lives. It takes time for data to become wisdom."[4] Muller sees the establishment of the Sabbath as God's provision for the time we need to accomplish this processing. I agree with Muller, but that is only a small part of what the Sabbath is about.

Evidently at the time of Jesus, the Romans despised the Jews for their day of rest. The Romans viewed it as a sign of laziness, though some did recognize its importance as physical refreshment and renewal for the week ahead. From the Jewish perspective, however, the Sabbath day is far more than a day of physical rest or a time to process mentally the data input of the previous week in hopes of turning it into wisdom—a view which is probably more Greek or Roman than Hebrew. For the Jews, Sabbath is *fundamental* to life and to both their *spiritual and emotional health.* It is the *culmination* of the week, the day that gives purpose to all other days.

Sabbath—A Glimpse into Eternity

The Jewish philosopher Abraham Heschel makes the miraculous and awe-inspiring quality of the Sabbath apparent. He calls it "one of life's highest rewards, a source of strength and inspiration to endure tribulation, to live nobly."[5] He goes on to explain that the ancient rabbis puzzled over the words in Genesis 2:2, "On the seventh day God *finished* his work" (ESV), which implied to them that there was an act of creation on the seventh day too. "What was created on the seventh day? *Tranquility, serenity, peace and repose.*"[6]

The rest of Sabbath is far more than withdrawal from labor and exertion. It is the rest and harmony of life as God intended it to be, an understanding that Howard Snyder equates with the biblical word *shalom,* which is God's ultimate goal of health and wholeness for all humankind and the whole of creation.

For Heschel, "The essence of the world to come is Sabbath eternal, and the seventh day in time is an example of eternity . . . a foretaste of the world to come."[7] What an incredible and revolutionary way to think of this important day. The Sabbath should shape and give substance to the rest of our week. One day out of every seven we have an opportunity to glimpse eternity, to experience the joy, tranquility, peace, and abundance of life as God intended it.

No wonder Jesus healed on the Sabbath. No wonder he constantly criticized the legalisms and restrictive rules the Pharisees inflicted on the people. Those rules robbed the people of the Sabbath's innate joy and freedom. Jesus wasn't downplaying the importance of Sabbath as a holy day; he was bringing the Jews an understanding of what Sabbath was meant to be, the culmination of their week and of their lives, the goal of all they gave their time to—a glimpse into eternity when all will be healed, fed, and supported. Imagine how different our lives would be if we viewed the Sabbath day from this perspective! It would be a pleasure—a day for experiencing the joy of fellowship with God, nurturing relationships with others, and enjoying the glories of God's creation.

Sabbath—God's Future Breaking into the Present

Christianity incorporated the spirit and beauty of the Sabbath into its theology. Most Christian traditions, however, transposed it to Sunday, the first day of the week and connected it to the resurrection of Jesus. Early Christians called this the "eighth" day. Since they believed God began creation on the first day, they thought Christ's rising on another first day centuries later meant that God was beginning a *new* creation. The Jews yearned for a future in which Sabbath was not just a day but a way of life seven days a week. In Christ, the early Christians believed that new world was opened to them.

"In coming together for collective worship on that sacred day, a day that signified the creation of the world, the resurrection of Christ, and the transcendence of ordinary time, Christians could imagine that they had already entered the new world promised at the end."[8] Just as the Sabbath was the culmination of the week for the Jews, so Sunday was to Christians what theologian Paul Stevens calls "a delicious relaxation in God"[9] and a preview of coming attractions. It is meant to be a day that *realigns our whole life,* reaffirming our relationship to God, God's Word, our families, others, and creation as well as to our work and study.

Stevens says, "In the New Testament, the Sabbath experienced in Jesus foreshadows the heavenly paradise where work and rest will be one glorious experience in the ultimate garden city, the New Jerusalem (Heb. 4:1–11). Our experience of Sabbath now, as followers of Jesus, is 'playing heaven.' Just as children imitate their parents and 'play house,' believers imitate their heavenly Father by anticipating and preparing for the ultimate environment that God has prepared for us."[10]

Orthodox Christians always viewed their church services as a preview of worship in heaven. Elaborate decoration welcomed worshipers into an environment that was meant to anticipate the glories of heaven. The liturgy was a grand rehearsal preparing Christians for the far grander experience of worship in heaven. Evidently back in the fourth century when Vladimir, Prince of Kiev, wanted to know which was the true religion, he sent his followers to explore various faiths. They found no joy until they arrived in Constantinople and attended St. Sophia, the heart of worship for orthodox Christians. Then they exclaimed, "We knew not whether we were in heaven or on earth."[11]

Orthodox Christians still see the church sanctuary as a foretaste of eternity. Worship is a glimpse of heaven on earth. The domed interior of an Orthodox church represents Christ's uniting of heaven and earth, which swallows up the day but opens a new world of opulent splendor and rich symbolism. The sanctuary is decorated with ornately carved panels, symbolizing the beauty of heaven. Incense represents the prayers and good works of the saints. Icons flicker in the candlelight, grained wood peeping under the cracks of aging red and gold and blue paint. Some icons date back to the fourteenth century and are representations of local saints meant to form a cloud of witnesses—fellow travelers, surrounding and encouraging us in our spiritual walk. The liturgy, the singing and chants, and above all the taking of communion focus the worshiper's experience on the wonder of Christ's sacrifice, the Lamb of God. In such a setting it is not hard to imagine that we are indeed glimpsing eternity and that God is walking once more in our midst.

I am not implying that we can bring the kingdom of God to earth by our efforts, but I do believe that our worship, joy in God's presence, and enjoyment of each other on the Sabbath give us glimpses of God's kingdom. We are meant to bring those glimpses into the lives of people around us so that they, like Prince Vladimir, can be unsure whether they are on earth or in heaven.

The Sabbath is a day to experience a foretaste of eternity—a day for playing heaven. It is a day not only to rest our bodies but also to enrich our souls and spirits, a day to recall with joy and gratitude the wonder of our salvation and God's redeeming activity in our lives and world. The Sabbath should shape and give rhythm to our week rather than our week shaping the kind of Sabbath we observe. The Sabbath gives priority to worship, fellowship with others, and enjoyment of God's creation. It is also a day for reflection, solitude, and study of the Word of God.

Sabbath Rest Becomes a Sunday To-Do List

Until recently, throughout most of the Christian world, Sunday *was* regarded as a day of rest. Shops and businesses closed. Families gathered for a time of renewal, spiritual refreshment, and celebration. Unfortunately we are just as prone to legalisms as were the Jews. For many Christians Sunday became a day of stringent religious observances with no fun or joy. It is often regarded more as a day that adds to our burdens than one that provides enjoyment and relaxation. On a trip to the north of Scotland a few years ago, I passed through a strict Presbyterian community that still ties down the children's swings on Saturday night so that they cannot be used on Sunday. In a predominately Dutch Reformed community in Iowa, we were told that new houses are always built with drains in the garage so that people can wash their cars on Sunday without being seen by their neighbors. What a tragedy if this is our view of eternity.

"Sunday to do list" proclaimed one advertisement in the *Seattle Times*. "Put on robe, open door, find Sunday newspaper waiting—for only $1.00." Sounds depressing to me, but reading the paper really is the highlight of Sunday mornings for many people. They view Sunday as a day to catch up on errands, make trips to the mall, and frantically transport kids to soccer and football games that are increasingly scheduled despite the conflict with church.

For Christians Sunday is often more stressful than other days as they juggle church commitments in their already overloaded schedules. Church adds to our stresses and pressures as committee meetings and church functions are often held on Sunday afternoons. I think more families argue before and on the way to church than at any other time during the week. Also, a growing percentage of the workforce toils on Sunday as more and more commerce beats to the 24/7 rhythm. There is certainly no time for the rest, refreshment, and fellowship to which the Sabbath calls us.

Reclaiming the Sabbath

I don't think there are any rigid rules for Sabbath keeping, and we certainly don't want to advocate the legalisms of the past. Flexibility needs to be the order of the day. As our situations change—kids are born, we change jobs, kids leave home, or we move—we need to reevaluate the practices we establish. Tilden Edwards, an Episcopal priest who has spent much time experimenting with Sabbath keeping, urges Christians to be flexible and creative in their embracing of a "Sabbath time" rather than a one-day-a-week observance. He recommends that Sunday be a time to combine worship with play and relaxation, and advocates adding a regular rhythm of disciplined spiritual renewal during the week.[12]

For many pastors and church workers, Sunday is the busiest day of the week. They often take their Sabbath on Saturday or Monday. In *Seven Days of Faith*, Paul Stevens suggests that for pastors, keeping the Jewish Sabbath could be most appropriate as Saturday is also often a day when spouses and children are at home—which makes possible their inclusion in the day's activities. Theologian Eugene Peterson and his wife find that Monday works best for them. They often go for a drive into the country, hike, read psalms, or spend a quiet evening at home.

For most of us Sunday is still the best day for Sabbath as that is the day that revolves around our churchgoing and our time of worship. For people who do need time on Sunday to prepare for the week ahead, starting on Saturday evening may be appropriate. By Sunday evening the Sabbath is over, and there is freedom to plan for the workweek. For others Sunday morning may be the time to start their rest. For those on shift work, the day on which Sabbath is observed may change weekly. When you get your work schedule, I think it is important to determine a week or two in advance when you will celebrate Sabbath. If you don't set aside that time well in advance, it will get consumed with other appointments. The early Celtic monks celebrated Sabbath on Saturday. Sunday—the day of resurrection—began the new life of the week. Sunday started with the Eucharist and celebration of Christ's resurrection. The rest of the day was a normal work day.[13]

Canadians John and Martha found that keeping Sabbath together with two active kids was a bit of a challenge. They decided to give each other a Sabbath break once a month for a day or two of prayer and reflection. The spouse not on Sabbath retreat spends time with the children. One of the unexpected byproducts is that both parents and kids appreciate each other more after they have been apart for a while. Another Canadian friend refuses to look at e-mail on Sunday—what he calls practicing an e-mail Sabbath.

Whether we celebrate Sabbath on Saturday, Sunday, or another day doesn't matter. What is important is that we *do* set aside a day as a holy Sabbath, not just to rest, refresh, and connect intimately to God but also to glimpse that eternal world for which we yearn. We can then allow the rest of our week and our commitments to be molded by that glimpse.

Running the Right Race

One of my favorite films is the Oscar award-winning *Chariots of Fire*. Eric Liddell, a devout Christian, is selected for the British Olympic team of 1928 and then discovers that his race will be held on a Sunday. He agonizes over this and finally decides that keeping the Lord's Day is far more important to him than the race. His decision hits the front pages of the newspaper, and huge pressure is exerted on him to change his mind—including a visit from the Prince of Wales. Against growing public anger, he stands by his convictions and refuses to run. At the last minute something incredible happens—one of his teammates who has already won a gold medal asks Eric to run in the 400 meters in his stead, and Eric Liddell wins a gold medal. This story impacted the lives of many in his day, and it still challenges the lives of those who watch the film almost a hundred years later.

Like Eric Liddell many of us feel that Sabbath keeping is against the growing pressures of our society. We make excuses why it is impossible to set aside one day a week as holy. Yet we too have no idea what is possible unless we try. When I first moved to the United States, I was shocked that shops were open on Sunday. I soon adjusted to this convenience and began shopping as much on Sunday as every other day.

In the last few years, however, Tom and I have made an active decision to avoid Sunday shopping so that it can truly be a day of rest from the secular world and a time of renewal. We have developed Sunday rituals that not only help us maintain this but also enable us to focus on God's purposes for our lives. Because we often travel on Sunday, our Sabbath keeping is very flexible. We have one set of routines when we are at home and another plan of action when we are on the road. A long overseas trip in particular challenges our creativity. In this situation we find that taking a couple of days for retreat often works better than trying to adhere to a one-day-in-seven Sabbath practice.

When we are at home, Sunday morning begins with coffee cake and a grande latté at our favorite restaurant. We journal and reflect on the past week. We share our joys, our encouraging moments, and our sense of fulfillment. We meditate on God's goodness and offer thanks for the rich blessings in our lives. Then we look at how we fulfilled God's call during the past week and discuss the upcoming week, setting goals for our use of time and resources. In the afternoon I try to spend an extended time in prayer and Bible study, refreshing my spirit and renewing myself for the week ahead. We have discovered that even if only every second week is committed to this schedule, our lives are both more relaxed and more focused on God's purposes.

I like Sunday as my Sabbath because it is the start of the week. It gives me the strong sense that I begin the week with God and all the work I commit myself to flows out of that relationship.

A Sabbath Celebration—Old Traditions, New Meaning

For my friend Dorothy, a converted Jew, the Sabbath has gained even greater significance. She began to observe the traditional Shabbat, beginning on Friday evening, when she was a college student at Yale and discovered that the practice brought her joy and a quiet perspective from which to examine the almost deafening demands of the academic world. When she became a Christian, she wished for a Christian equivalent to the traditions and communal feeling of this beautiful Jewish ceremony.

Years later when a good friend offered to celebrate with her, she worried, "Is it really kosher for a Christian to enjoy this Jewish ritual?" She was thrilled, however, as he explained the prayers to her.

After she prayed the Hebrew words over the candles, he said, "If Mary did not say this same prayer, she would at least have prayed its precursor."

Then her friend lifted the bread, the *challah,* and blessed it. He broke off a piece, ate it, and handed another piece to her. Dorothy was struck by the relationship between the Sabbath seder (meal) and the Christian communion service. "I was profoundly moved to see how in the *Shabbat* ceremony ordinary people—mothers and fathers—become priests, blessing the food they provide for their families, making space for the sacred around their own tables," she said. "I gained new admiration for the mission of the church, which in providing communion to so many at once announces its intention to regard all those as one intimate family. The more I experience the Jewish Sabbath, the more impressed I am with it and with Jesus."

For Bill Child, chairman of R. C. Willey Home Furnishings and a devout Mormon, Sunday is also a holy day—and the day that shapes how he lives throughout the week. His chain of furniture stores is never open on Sunday. When he decided to sell his business to billionaire Warren Buffett and they wanted to open a store in Boise, Idaho, Child's practice was challenged because 20 to 30 percent of all furniture sales are made on Sunday. Child insisted on paying for the new store himself with the proviso that the store close on Sunday. If the Boise store took hold, he would sell it back to Warren Buffett at cost; if it failed, he would eat the losses. The store thrived, and Child contends that it is because the Sunday closure enables him to attract workers who want to spend the day with family.[14] Making the decision to keep the

Sabbath may mean making sacrifices or being challenged, but it will also leave a lasting impression on our lives and those around us.

Shaping the Sabbath—The Rest of Accomplishment

What should shape our Sabbath day? Obviously, as the examples above suggest, there are many possibilities. There are two important guidelines for us to follow.

First, the Sabbath is meant to be a day of rest from weekly toil but not primarily as refreshment in preparation for the week ahead. In Exodus, the Sabbath is connected to God's rest after creating the world. It is not just a rest from work; *it is the rest of accomplishment,* when God looked at all creation with satisfaction and walked among it with enjoyment. "God saw all that he had made, and it was very good. And there was evening, and there was morning—the sixth day. Thus the heavens and the earth were completed in all their vast array. By the seventh day God had finished the work he had been doing; so on the seventh day he rested from all his work. And God blessed the seventh day and made it holy, because on it he rested from all the work of creating that he had done" (Gen. 1:31–2:2).

For us too Sabbath is meant to be a holy day, a day to rest in the joy of God's presence. It is a time to glimpse that coming attraction—when Christ returns and an eternal Sabbath rest comes for all creation. It is a time to look back in satisfaction and fulfillment at all we have accomplished the preceding week to fulfill our purpose as representatives of God's kingdom.

It is *not* a time to look ahead to what still needs to be accomplished. This is something that I have not always found easy. I love to plan new projects and am often looking ahead to my next task before I have finished the current one—which tends to create the feeling that I never quite measure up. No matter how much I do, there is always a task ahead of me.

This was a particular burden when I was medical director on the mercy ship *Anastasis*. I continually focused on our next port. I lived with constant heartache for the people I met whose faces were distorted by enormous tumors and was overwhelmed by the needs of people who lacked even basic health care. I never took time to relax.

Eventually I realized I needed to "slow down and smell the roses." I had to relax and delight in the lives that had already been touched and transformed as we performed cleft lip and palate and eye surgeries. I started going down to the post-op ward to watch the patients as their bandages were removed. It was like a Sabbath experience for me. I watched them gaze into a mirror at their transformed faces and drank in their joy as their faces lit with radiant smiles. Not only were they transformed but also I basked in the delight that God obviously took in what we were doing. Listening to the stories of patients who had often traveled for hundreds of miles to receive their surgeries was even more fulfilling when I viewed these in the light of God's eternal kingdom.

Shaping the Sabbath—Remembrance and Gratitude

The second tip to remember for shaping the Sabbath is that it is meant to be a day of *remembrance and gratitude* for our own redemption and freedom. In Deuteronomy, the Sabbath is rooted in the remembrance of the Israelites' liberation from slavery in Egypt. "On it you shall not do any work, neither you, nor your son, or daughter, nor your manservant or maidservant, nor your ox, your donkey or any of your animals, nor the alien within your gates, so that your manservant and maidservant may rest, as you do. Remember that you were slaves in Egypt and that the LORD your God brought you out of there with a mighty hand and an outstretched arm. Therefore the LORD your God has commanded you to observe the Sabbath day" (Deut. 5:14–15).

As a young doctor I seriously considered becoming a psychiatrist and spent a year working as a psychiatric resident at Christchurch Hospital in New Zealand. Most of our patients were teenage girls who had taken overdoses or slashed their wrists in an attempt at suicide. One evening as I hovered over my third overdose patient for the day, I caught a flash of myself at the same age. I was often depressed and struggled with worthlessness just like these young women. At the age of sixteen I became a Christian and my life was transformed. "This is what God saved me from," I thought. I was overwhelmed by an intense feeling of gratitude. Even today, the memory of that scene fills me with joy and thanksgiving for God's salvation. Sabbath should be a time to look back with gratitude for our freedom in Christ. It is a day to exult in the liberty and wholeness we experience through Christ as well as a day to reach and extend that wholeness to others.

Out of our gratitude for God's redemption and freedom should flow other aspects of Sabbath keeping—a longing to join in worship with other people of faith as well as a desire to see the rest of humankind set free as we have been. This is a day for fellowship and hospitality, a time to embrace God and our community, particularly those who would normally be excluded or rejected. It is also a day for generosity when we express through our monetary gifts our gratitude and thankfulness to God for the many blessings bestowed on us. And last, the Sabbath is a time for enjoying God's creation and the beauty around us.

Tragically research in the last few years has suggested that three major areas of our lives have suffered as society encourages us to spend more time inside at work and online—our time at church, our time with others, and our time outside enjoying God's creation. All of them provide such crucial ways for us to connect to God and his purposes. Reinstating the Sabbath is one way to reestablish these priorities and enrich our lives.

A Sabbath Rhythm

In her wonderful book *Keeping the Sabbath Wholly,* theologian Marva Dawn provides a comprehensive look at the many aspects of Sabbath. She divides the Sabbath observance into four main categories, which you may like to consider as you plan your own Sabbath rituals. She sees it as a day of *ceasing*—from work, worry, anxiety, and most importantly from trying to be God. It is a day of *resting*—physically, emotionally, intellectually, and spiritually. It is a day of *embracing*—our community through offering hospitality, personal wholeness, and our call or purpose in the world. It is a day of *feasting*—on God, music, beauty, creation, food, affection, and celebration. She says, "To decide that you will keep the Sabbath is the most important starting point, and to continue faithful in that decision even though you are tempted to break it will reap a harvest of blessings."[15]

Focus-on-the-Family Rhythm Too

There are many ways in which we can make this day special—a time of celebration and reflection for ourselves and our families. The lighting of candles, the retelling of family history, or the telling of biblical stories are all traditions that can relax and help us intentionally focus on God and the beautiful rhythm of his eternal world. In *Making Sunday Special,* Karen Burton Mains gives rich suggestions for family observances that mirror the Jewish Sabbath rituals.[16] I think it is still one of the best resources available for shaping family Sabbath observances. Sara Wenger Shenk's book *Why Not Celebrate!* is another excellent resource that provides two liturgies for a Sabbath celebration that were regularly used by families at the Mennonite community Reba Place.[17]

Celtic Daily Prayer, which provides a rich array of prayers and devotional readings from the Northumbria community situated near Holy Island off the east coast of England, also includes a Sabbath liturgy with a Celtic flavor.[18] They suggest that the use of the Sabbath meal and ritual does not need to be restricted to a Sabbath day observance. It can also be used at the beginning of any meal with family or friends. One beautiful suggestion they make is that we leave one spare place setting or seat at the table to welcome Christ, who comes in the guise of the stranger or unexpected visitor. "This reminds us that we long for the coming of Christ—His return—and yet honor His presence with us. Also, it teaches us to treat with honor whoever may come and be given the place prepared as His [Christ's]."[19] They also point out that because the Sabbath celebration traditionally begins with the women presiding over the prayers of blessing for the family, honoring women as well as men is an important aspect of the celebration.[20]

For Mark and Judy, Sunday dinner has become a family ritual that provides a time of fellowship and bonding for the family. It is also an opportunity to look outward and focus on people in need in the local community and around the world. The family prays together for friends and missionaries around the world and for those who have been devastated by earthquakes, hurricanes, droughts, or war. They also thank God for his provision and for the answers they have seen to last week's prayers. This has become a very important time for their son, Christopher, who has found tremendous security in knowing God does care for him, his family, and the hurting world.

A Beginning and an End

Marva Dawn suggests, "To set the day apart, it is important to establish a precise, deliberate beginning and ending."[21] This is great advice for all of us—a definite time at which we put the worries of the week to rest and focus on the Sabbath. I can think of no better way to do this than with one of the traditional Jewish prayers for Sabbath eve:

> Come, let us welcome the Sabbath in joy and peace! Like a bride, radiant and joyous, comes the Sabbath. It brings blessings to our hearts; workday thoughts and cares are put aside. The brightness of the Sabbath light shines forth to tell that the divine spirit of love abides within our home. In that light all our blessings are enriched, all our griefs and trials are softened.[22]

Starting our day with a simple prayer savoring the joy and peace of God's presence and actively clearing our minds of our workday cares and concerns can bring tremendous freedom.

To end the day, consider another prayer that looks forward to the next Sabbath and the eternal rest God promises at Christ's return. "The Jews bid goodbye to the Sabbath with final prayers that include a pang of longing for its next appearance seven days later. When we live for our Sabbaths, when they are the climax of our weeks, we know a healthy anticipation of the ultimate rest, the time when Jesus will come to take us home."[23] You may like to use one of these traditional prayers or create your own prayer. Below is my rendition of a prayer that focuses on that eternal Sabbath for which I yearn and on those around me who are unable to rest because of hunger, oppression, or illness.

> As we close this Sabbath day, O God, we come longing for
>   your future to be revealed,
> In a world polluted and destroyed, we remember you
>   promise renewal for all creation,
> Your Sabbath rest is all inclusive.
> In a world where many are heavy laden, you promise to
>   take our yoke upon you,
> Your Sabbath rest shares our burdens.
> In a world where many are imprisoned and persecuted,
>   you promise to set the captives free,
> Your Sabbath rest frees from oppression.
> In a world where many are starving, you promise to feed
>   the hungry,
> Your Sabbath rest provides abundance for all.
> In a world where many are diseased and disabled you
>   promise to heal the sick,
> Your Sabbath rest brings us wholeness.
> We live in anticipation of that day when Christ returns, and
>   a Sabbath rest comes for all peoples,
> Not alone but as part of a great international community
>   that is your body.
> Maranatha, come, Lord Jesus, come into our hearts and
>   our lives,
> And grant us your eternal Sabbath rest.

Listen to the Beat—Let's Glimpse Eternity

As I worked on the research for this chapter, I was deeply convicted by what I read. I realized how little I understood the meaning of Sabbath. My Sundays were often stress-filled days dedicated to catching up or preparing for a busy week. Until recently, observing Sabbath was not a priority, and I still struggle with knowing how to fully integrate its meaning into my life.

I am challenged by the idea of entering into the joy of Sabbath as a glimpse of eternity. Taking the Sabbath seriously affects the rhythm and focus of my whole life, not just one day a week. I can't glimpse eternity and ignore oppression and injustice or be complacent about the plight of people starving in Africa. I can't truly celebrate the Sabbath when I am angry with my brothers and sisters or my colleagues. Even when I ignore the homeless and disregard the plight of the poor in my community, it is difficult to enter into the spirit of God's Sabbath rest. If people in my community are unable to celebrate Sabbath because they do not receive a living wage and must work seven days a week, how should I help them? What is my responsibility for the needs I see?

Sabbath is not something we celebrate alone or for a moment—it is living to a new rhythm in anticipation of that day when Christ returns and all are made whole. "Receiving *this* day, after all, means joining in the song of creation, which renews our love for the earth and our gratitude for the blessings God grants through it. Receiving *this* day means joining in the worldwide song of liberation, a song whose vibrations cut through our own forms of bondage and awaken us to the need of all people for freedom and justice. Receiving *this* day means singing *Alleluia* and being renewed in faith, hope and love. It is the eighth day, and the future God has promised is breaking in. No other days can be the same after this one."[24]

---

1. Spend a few moments meditating on the concept of Sabbath as a glimpse into eternity, an opportunity to "play heaven."

Write a short paragraph or poem, or draw a picture that depicts how you would like to spend your day.

2. What prayers, rituals, and celebrations could you develop to make your present Sabbath observances look more like your ideal?

3. What one step could you take in the next month to move toward these goals?

8

THE RHYTHM OF CHRISTMAS

*J*n Ethiopia, where Christianity can be traced back
almost two thousand years, the Christmas season is a
time for great celebration and ceremony. Thousands
make the pilgrimage to Lalibela, a village where thirteenth-
century Coptic Christians built eleven churches underground
to avoid persecution.[1] Some worshipers walk for days, weeks,
or even months to spend Christmas Day in this holy place.
They pause regularly by the roadside for prayer and meditation and at night hunch over the Bible, reading in the dim
light of a flickering candle. Christmas Eve is an all-night vigil
illuminated by candles and highlighted by singing, dancing,
and prayer.

Christmas Day is a time for pageantry and joyful celebration. Processions parade through the streets, their participants

richly clad in flowing African robes embroidered with gold thread. Singers and dancers herald the approach of colorful Christmas icons and richly decorated nativity scenes. At Lalibela worshipers gather around one of the ancient churches sculpted out of the pinkish rock and share breakfast together. Each person kisses an ornate cross that is passed through the crowd. They sing and dance and worship God. The service lasts several hours and culminates in a feast, where families slaughter and cook a goat.[2]

A Rhythm of Feast and Fast

In addition to daily and weekly rhythms, we need to reconnect to God in our yearly cycle of life. Until recently, Christianity was always a faith with a yearly rhythm of joyous celebration and enthusiastic worship punctuated by periods of fasting and serious reflection. This rhythm was inherited from the Jewish cycle of feasting and festival, which has its roots in the biblical story of the Old Testament.

Christians gave new significance to these biblical feasts. Passover was transformed into Easter, and *Shavuot,* the festival held between the end of the barley harvest and beginning of the wheat harvest, gave rise to Pentecost. Over the centuries other feasts and festivals of unique importance were added, the most important being Christmas Day.[3]

For Christians throughout the last two thousand years, the celebrations of Christmas and Easter provided pivotal points for community life, as demonstrated by the wonderful Christmas festivities in Ethiopia. The cycle of feasting and fasting that was once so integral to the practice of Christianity gave rise to what is now known as the Christian calendar. As our society has become more secular, however, we have forgotten or ignored these historic yearly rhythms.

These seasons should *still* provide *focal points* for the celebration of our faith, and our whole year should *still* flow to a rhythm of *feasting and fasting* that very deliberately reminds us of the biblical events that shape our beliefs. Connecting to the joy and despair of the biblical story through a rhythm of feasts and fasts can be rejuvenating whether we are a part of a traditional liturgical church or not.

In the next three chapters we will look at how we can reconnect to this yearly rhythm and establish new and meaningful rituals. In this chapter we will explore how we can more fully enter into the celebrations of the Christmas season—Advent, Christmas, and Epiphany. In the next chapter we will look at the Easter cycle—Lent, Easter, and Pentecost. Finally, in the last chapter we will discuss creative ways that you and your family can establish a cycle of feasting and fasting that brings a faith-based rhythm to all the events of your year and to the cycle of your life.

The Rhythm of Wholeness

Why do we need this rhythm of feasting and fasting? Donna Fletcher Crow, in *Seasons of Prayer: Rediscovering Classic Prayers through the Christian Calendar,* suggests that the church calendar provides a whole different way of keeping track of time and enables us to live in the gospel story on a daily basis. "To observe the passage of each year by remembering and walking through Christ's ministry on earth is in a small way to live our days here as he lived them."[4] To live throughout the year with a rhythm that reminds us of Christ's life and ministry is a wonderful thought and an incredible opportunity.

Worship leader Robert Webber contends that this is part of what makes us different from the secular community. He says that for Christians, the rhythm of the year is meant to be governed by the life, death, and resurrection of Jesus, not by the civil and national holidays of our country or by the dictates of the consumer culture in which we live.[5] By connecting to the seasons of the church year, we enter into a rhythm that focuses every day and every season very intentionally on the One who gives life meaning and purpose.

More than that, as Gertrud Mueller Nelson expresses it, "By celebrating through the structures of the Church we actually are given *the forms* we need to become *whole* and we are given *the formulas* to make whole *every* human experience. This effort requires our rediscovery of the themes which the cycles of the church calendar offer us and the application of our creative imagination to the rites and folk customs already available. Then, through the celebration of the sacred mysteries, we will find new meaning in the inexplicable and a worthy container for what we realize in our hearts" (emphasis added).[6] To be made whole, to find health and healing for our minds, bodies, and souls, and even our communities, that is what we crave.

The amazing thing is that such healing is possible—not through repeated trips to the doctor or through the downing of a handful of pills. Healing comes as we walk with Christ through the *joy and pain* of his life, death, and resurrection. By *joining* with Christ, our lives are transformed and we experience wholeness that no other way of life can provide. Even more amazingly, as we are transformed, we become God's *instruments of healing* and wholeness for others and for his creation.

The World Loves to Party

Not surprisingly, our secular culture abounds with occasions to indulge our love of festivity and celebration. It entices us into its festivals with the promise that they will bring the health and wholeness we crave. Joy, Intimacy, and Passion are marketed as exotic perfumes that hold the elusive promises of fulfillment for our hopes and emotions. Aromatherapy uses incense and soothing bath salts to caress us and wash away our cares. The soothing tones of fountains and water sculptures promise to quiet our jangling nerves. Prozac, with its promised tranquility, has become one of the most commonly prescribed medications of our Western world.

The consumer culture even tries to provide a quasi-religious rhythm to its seasons. One young woman bounced up to me after a recent seminar and exclaimed, "I have a liturgical rhythm to my life. There is the pre-Christmas sale, the after-Christmas sale, the Easter sale, and the Thanksgiving sale." She wasn't kidding! She confided with embarrassment that her life was defined by these seasonal events. They provided the pivotal points for her year.

Discovering a Shalom Rhythm for Your Life

Tom and I are Anglicans come lately. We did not grow up with a liturgical church tradition. Only in the last few years have we discovered the richness of the church calendar and the beautiful meaning it gives to yearly seasons and patterns. Growing up in Australia where we celebrate Christmas in the middle of summer and Easter at the beginning of autumn, I was even more disconnected from the relevance of these seasons than most westerners. It was hard to think about resurrection when everything around me was dying, and Christmas on the beach at the height of summer didn't seem relevant to those frosty nights mentioned in Christmas carols.

Then I spent a winter in Victoria, British Columbia, during one of the coldest seasons on record. For the first time I enjoyed the breathless expectation of Advent when everything around me was slumbering, waiting in anticipation of the birth of the one who brought new life into the world. I watched the world come alive as spring burst forth in all its glory and Easter approached. The snowdrops poked their heads through the chilly ground, and the daffodils turned their bright yellow faces toward the warming sun, heralding the coming of spring with the promise of resurrection. It was not hard for me to imagine Christ bursting from his tomb with the promise of resurrection life for all humankind.

To those who did not grow up with a liturgical tradition, the idea that living by the rhythm of the church calendar can bring health and wholeness may sound far-fetched. However, it is usually through the events of the church calendar—Advent, Christmas, Lent, and Easter—that we connect to religious rituals and symbols for the inner healing Christ gives. The rituals of confession of sin and repentance, foot washing and baptism, anointing with oil, and communion give physical expression to our suffering and healing and in so doing bridge the gap between our personal experiences and the meaning of the gospel story. Even the simple act of eating with others or praying together can be a concrete event that cements the healing of reconciliation for people who were estranged because of misunderstanding, prejudice, or violence.

Each year has two Christ-centered cycles that begin with a season of reflection and preparation followed by a time of celebration and rejoicing. Advent prepares us for the joy of Christmas and Epiphany, and Lent ushers in the wonders of Easter and Pentecost.[7] The remaining six months of the year are usually called ordinary time—the time without festivals—though I prefer the more inspiring term *Kingdomtide*. This is the season "when we get down to garden growing and Kingdom building."[8] During this time we can focus on the life of the church and its mission and create our own celebrations to share the joy of resurrection life with those around us.

Breaking the Power of Eternal Winter

Unfortunately just as Protestants threw out the liturgy at the Reformation, we also discarded the pageants and processions that heralded the celebration of our faith and provided a tangible pathway for healing and nurture. As liturgy and ritual were slowly marginalized, so were all other external symbols of religiosity—candles, icons, incense, crosses, processions, and celebrations of religious festivals.

"John Calvin, a Swiss reformer, felt that ceremonious religion presented an obstacle to true worship and that attention should focus instead on one God who is Spirit. Since God's self is revealed to us in the Bible, in language, the Puritan reformers felt that it is through words alone that we should pray to and adore God."[9] The Puritans in England even banned the celebration of Christmas and the baking of festive fruit mince pies, traditionally shaped in ovals to represent the manger in which Jesus slept. Those wily Brits, not to be denied their celebrations, surreptitiously baked square pies that would not be recognized by the Puritans![10]

Perhaps this was what C. S. Lewis had in mind when he created his mythical land of Narnia. In *The Lion, the Witch and the Wardrobe*, C. S. Lewis's classic fantasy novel, Lucy discovers she can enter the snow-shrouded land of Narnia through the back of a wardrobe. Narnia is an intriguing place inhabited not by humans but by talking animals. Lucy is befriended by Mr. Tumnus, a faun, who lets her in on a terrible secret. Narnia is a somber place because it is under the spell of the white witch. It is a place, she is told, "where it is always winter and never Christmas."[11] It is a place with no joy, no feasting, and no celebration. Into this cold and somber land comes Aslan, the great lion, who alone is able to break the power of the white witch and her hold of eternal winter. As her power dwindles, Christmas arrives and the animals begin to feast and celebrate. Then spring breaks out. As Aslan moves through the land, grass and wildflowers burst forth from under his feet in a riotous, exultant celebration of new life.

It is true that religious ceremonies and festivals are an inadequate way to worship God and we all need an understanding of Scripture to anchor our faith. However, just as Aslan brought festivity and celebration to the land of Narnia, so Christ is meant to break the power of the eternal winter of our souls and bring festivity and celebration to our lives.

Fast Before the Feast

The rhythm of the church year is not just about feasting. As we reconnect to joyous celebrations, we must learn to fast as well. I don't think it is possible to fully appreciate the lavish feasts of Easter and Christmas or to experience the wholeness these events should bring to our lives unless we have fasted beforehand. "When affluence allows people to feast too frequently and independently of others, feasting loses its joy and integrity. It results in ill health and dulls our sensitivity to the needs of others. . . . Reserving for special events foods we might easily afford, but that are luxury items in the world economy, unites us with those who have less."[12] Fasting and "doing without" helps connect us to another part of God's story—the pain and anguish that Christ willingly took upon himself because of his identification with human suffering.

Most of us want to avoid pain and suffering at all costs. Advertisements convince us that we "haven't got time for pain," and so we expect instant cures for headaches, colds, and even cancer. When we don't find relief, we become angry and resentful—often toward God, who we feel allows us to suffer unjustly. Paul Brand, a gifted surgeon who worked with leprosy patients in India, views pain and suffering in a different light. Having spent much of his career working with people who are deprived of the sensation of pain, he feels that "pain is one of the most remarkable design features of the human body, and if I could choose one gift for my leprosy patients it would be the gift of pain."[13] People who insist on having every vestige of pain removed often move around too quickly and break open their wounds. Those that refuse to move because it hurts don't fully recover either and in the intricate work of hand surgery that Dr. Brand is involved in, this can mean that they end up with stiff joints and permanent incapacity.

Pain has a purpose. If we try to do away with it or if we pretend that the traumas of our lives have never occurred, then we too are incapacitated. We become stiff and immovable in body, mind, and spirit. Only when we willingly walk with Jesus through the joy *and* suffering of life will we discover the wonder of a compassionate caring God who bears our pain and grief.

Waiting for the birth of Christ at Christmas can be synonymous with our own waiting for relief from depression or despair. As we enter into the agony and horror of Christ's crucifixion on Good Friday, we may be able to face the horrors of our own grief, abandonment, and pain. Then as we exult in the joy of Easter morning, we share the healing power of Christ's resurrection that promises hope and health for our broken and dead places.

This doesn't mean that we should actively seek out suffering. Self-flagellation and asceticism is not God's intention. But facing our pain and suffering often opens our eyes to the suffering of others—to deprivation and oppression that are beyond our comprehension. Hopefully, as we will discuss more in the following chapter, it encourages us to "bear one another's burdens" (Gal. 6:2 NASB) and to "look not only to your own interests, but also to the interests of others" (Phil. 2:4). It draws us into solidarity with their struggles and prompts us to reach out to relieve their pain and include them in our feasting.

Advent—The Promise of Things to Come

The Christian calendar begins at the end of November, with the season of Advent. This is a season not only of refreshment and renewal but also of refocusing as we contemplate the birth of the one who brings life and meaning to all we are and do. We await the coming of Christ in quiet anticipation. We don't just await his coming to us as a baby. We also remember his coming as a Savior to any who will receive him, and in breathless anticipation we await his coming again at the end of time when God will make all things new.

Advent begins, at least in the Northern Hemisphere, at the darkest time of the year when the world seems to sleep—and many of us feel like sleeping. It invites us to accept the natural rhythms of our body and not to fight against them. It encourages us to slow down—to rest, reflect, and refocus. In so doing it allows us time to grieve the pains and agonies of life and find healing.

I have never been more aware of the healing nature of this season than in 2001 following the horrific events of September 11 and the thousands of deaths at the World Trade Center. As the daylight hours shortened, I found myself longing for the beginning of Advent. In its quiet moments I was able to grieve and to process the appalling images that had flashed time and time again across television screens. The reflective time of Advent enabled me to move beyond wanting revenge and retribution. As I walked toward the commemoration of his birth, I was reminded that Christ came into our world because of evil. He came to take our sufferings and pain upon himself. As I identified with Christ's sufferings, I drew closer to the pain and suffering of others—not only victims of terrorism but also of hunger, oppression, and injustice.

Unplug the Christmas Tree

I don't think there is any starker contrast in our world than between the focus of the Christian calendar during Advent and the secular hype of the pre-Christmas season. The two rhythms are completely opposite. People rush frantically through the crowded malls laden down with everything from Santa dollhouses to Moses nutcracker toys. An igloo playhouse vies with wooden nativity sets for our attention. A barrage of psychedelic stimuli and raucous music encourages us to spend more, eat more, and party more. One advertisement even suggests that "praises will be heard on high" when we eat chocolate royale cheesecake. Recently a friend confided, "I hate Christmas. It is the most pressurized, stressed-out time of the year for me. I spend far too much money, eat far too much food, and constantly worry about whether I have forgotten to buy a gift for someone important. There is so much to do, I don't even have time to think about Christ's birth let alone celebrate his coming into the world."

For many people, the pre-Christmas season *is* the hardest time of the year—and not just because they overindulge. Often the cultural atmosphere of the season is totally out of synch with the rhythm of our bodies and our spirits. The short days of winter make us want to slow down and join the animals in hibernation. This is the season when we remember loved ones who have died and grieve our separation from them. During this season we are most vulnerable to loneliness and despair, particularly if we are struggling with divorce or broken family relationships. Depression is at its height, made more acute by the contrasting images of merrymaking around us.

Since there is no time to grieve, no time to refocus, and no time to experience that much-needed healing a season of reflection can bring, our lives suffer. One church in Ottawa holds a "Blue Christmas service," which acknowledges the pressures that people feel. This service is a far more authentic reflection of how many of us experience this season and is much more in keeping with its spiritual meaning.

Living the Joy of the Season

Tom has always been a Christmas person. He was absolutely delighted when he discovered the liturgical calendar and that Christmas is meant to be a long rich season of celebration. Christmas is no longer just a day. It extends from the beginning of Advent four weeks before Christmas, through Christmas Day, the twelve days of Christmas, and finally into Epiphany, which commemorates the coming of the three wise men. We can use all of these events as the focus for family and community celebrations.

We buy our Christmas tree and decorate our house at the beginning of Advent. We put lights in the windows and red and green Christmas mats on the furniture. We scatter rich, vibrant poinsettias in red and pink and white throughout the house. In our living room we set up a nativity scene and adorn our dining room table with an Advent wreath. Four bright red candles nestle in a bed of greenery around a central white candle.

At breakfast each morning we light the candles, symbolic of Christ as our light in the darkness of the world. During the first week of Advent we light only one candle. Each week we light an additional candle. Finally, on Christmas Day we light the central candle as well, and we keep them all lit throughout the twelve days of Christmas. As the candles burn brightly, we read the daily Scriptures from *The Book of Common Prayer* and focus on our celebration of Christ's birth. This short ritual refocuses my energy on my faith at this busy season and brings tremendous refreshment and renewal to my spirit. I have adapted a few lines of liturgy that I like to read as a prelude to lighting the candles:

> As quietly as the winter steals upon us, the season of joy approaches.
> We wait for our Redeemer, for God's love to come in fullness
> As candlelight overcomes the darkness, so your light radiates within us
> For light penetrates the darkness and prepares the way of the Lord.

Since we began celebrating Advent like this, Christmas shopping has lost its appeal. The glitz and glitter of the malls is so stridently opposed to my focus on waiting and listening that I hate to go near them. I do my gift buying before December, which has many advantages including less crowded and quieter shops.

Advent—Coming Home to the Kingdom of God

For Tom and me, Advent is not just a time of quiet reflection. We also love to enter into the party atmosphere by holding an annual Advent celebration. Its focus is the anticipation of the return of Christ and that great and joyous homecoming of God when people from every tribe and nation will walk together to the banquet feast that God has prepared. Sometimes we read the passages out of Isaiah that speak of that great homecoming. We rejoice in the imagery of release from poverty and oppression in Isaiah 58:5–9 and the wonder of healing as crutches are thrown down, wheelchairs are discarded, and the eyes of the blind are opened in Isaiah 35:5–6. We delight in the dance of God's restored creation in Isaiah 35:1–3, and imagine the wonder of a world without pain, suffering, and death as promised in Isaiah 9:2–7.

Sometimes we draw pictures that bring to life the richness of that banquet feast and the incredible celebration of that shalom future of God when everything is made whole. On other occasions we dance or sing. Sometimes we light candles and sit quietly, reflecting on the coming of Christ into our midst.

Then we begin our own banquet feast, serving dishes from around the world that reflect the vast array of tastes and aromas God has created. I always start with my own traditional Christmas fare—Scottish shortbread and English Christmas cake. To these we add *hoummus* and *Baba Ghannouj* from the Middle East, a wonderful cheese ball from Italy, hors d'oeuvres from Asia, a tropical fruit plate, and a vast array of Christmas pastries and cookies from Greek, Swedish, Australian, and American cultures. We end the evening, as we believe we will begin our eternal homecoming, with the bread and wine of communion.

Advent—A Family Event

Advent is a wonderful tradition to celebrate as a family where the lighting of the Advent wreath and the reading of Scripture may be done before or after dinner or just before bedtime. As Sara Wenger Shenk suggests in *Why Not Celebrate!* every member of the family can be given a part to play in the celebration. One child may light the candles; another may snuff them out. Someone else may read the Scripture, offer a prayer, or choose an Advent song or devotional reading.[14] Shenk also gives instructions for creating an Advent calendar and Advent wreath. In keeping with the reflective spirit of the season you may like to set aside an evening a week for each member of the family to reflect on the painful events of the year both in their lives and across the world. At the end of each evening these can be offered to God in a time of healing prayer.

Another excellent resource is *Celebrating the Christian Year* by Martha Zimmerman. She provides ideas on how to celebrate other family-oriented festivals that fall during the Advent season. St. Nicholas Day is a favorite among my Dutch friends. It provides an alternative to extravagant gift giving at Christmas. St. Lucia Day is an important celebration for those of Scandinavian background, and St. Lucia can provide a wonderful role model for young women. Lucia was a young Italian woman who lived in the third century A.D. She was meant to marry a pagan but gave her dowry away as a public declaration of her Christian faith. That deed was so strange that people thought she was possessed by evil spirits. She was martyred in A.D. 304. "She is called the 'Queen of Lights' because she was willing to give up her life to honor Christ. Lucy boldly held high the light of Christ for all to see at a time in history when that was not popular."[15] These feasts can provide excellent opportunities to punctuate the solemnity of reflection with times of fun and celebration, a very necessary relief for children, and in fact for all of us at this season.

For Steve and Anne, Advent has always been a time of renewal and family bonding. When their kids were small, they read Bible stories each night, starting in Genesis and moving all the way through into the Gospels. After each story, the kids grabbed a sheet of paper and some crayons to illustrate their understanding of what had been said. They posted the brightly colored pictures on the walls, slowly filling the house with the biblical story as they followed the children of Israel out of Egypt and into the Promised Land. Finally, they read the story of Jesus' coming into the world, reliving once again the wonder and awe of this momentous event.

Steve and Anne open presents and celebrate Christmas as a family on Christmas Eve. Christmas Day is then a time to give Christmas away, to give a gift to Jesus as they provide a meal for some of the needy and lonely people in their neighborhood who have no one else to care for them.

Christmas—Celebrating the Birth of Christ

Christmas is probably the most widely celebrated Christian festival in the world. Incredibly the birth of a tiny baby two thousand years ago in an obscure village in Judea still has the power to impact and transform lives. Unfortunately it is fast losing its religious significance, as it has become the most commercialized event on our calendars. Even people with little or no religious belief send cards and exchange presents. Sometimes enemies call a truce, and on occasion those involved in active warfare stop killing for the duration of Christmas Day.

Those of us of Christian faith, however, should never forget that we *are* celebrating the birth of our Savior. Martha Zimmerman explains, "Christmas was established to celebrate the 'Incarnation,' God becoming human in order to be 'at one' with us."[16] That doesn't mean we should try to out-party the partyers, but it does mean we should focus our celebrations on the coming of the Prince of Peace and all the implications that this has for our lives both now and in the eternal world to come. At this season in particular we are called to bring love, joy, and peace into the world.

Unplug the Christmas Machine: A Guide to Putting Love and Joy Back into Your Holiday Celebration is an excellent resource that gives creative suggestions for celebrations with religious meaning and purpose. Another good resource is Alternatives for Simple Living, an organization dedicated to "help people challenge the way our consumer society continues to usurp our holy days and exploit people and the environment." Their catalog and web site provide many wonderful ideas for how we can give this season a more Christ-centered focus. Some of these ideas can be downloaded directly from their web site (www.simpleliving.org).

One suggestion I find particularly appealing is to give 25 percent of what you spent last year on gifts, to the poor.[17] A number of Christian relief and development agencies have alternative gift catalogs that enable donors to contribute angora rabbits, woolly sheep, or goats to needy families around the world—not just providing for their immediate needs but giving them an opportunity to develop resources for their ongoing support. A Presbyterian church in Pennsylvania has really entered into the spirit of this alternative giving. For several weeks before Christmas, certain members bring goats, rabbits, and sheep into the church parking lot and foyer so members can get an idea of what they are contributing.

Another possibility is to give the gift of time off to someone who is a caregiver for a physically or emotionally disabled person. Or you may like to give the gift of fun and festivity to people who normally have little cheer. For the last few years, our church has provided a Christmas banquet for a local women's shelter. Mountains of food, gifts for the kids, and a preview of the church's Christmas pageant have made this a memorable occasion for everyone.

Perhaps like Tom and Kim and their two sons, Jared and Eric, you could give the gift of Christmas to people who are lonely or separated from their families. Participating in the

InterVarsity Christian Fellowship International Christmas event has been a highlight of their Christmas season. Sharing Christmas with students from around the world, many of whom have never experienced it before, has given the boys a passion for God's people in lands across the globe.

Celebrating the Christmas Story

One of my favorite TV shows is *The Vicar of Dibley,* a British sitcom that revolves around the life of a woman vicar in a small rural community in England. At Christmas she decides to provide an authentic Christmas pageant for her parish at a local farm using live animals. The reenactment turns out to be a little more realistic than she intended, however, as her best friend proceeds to give birth to her first child among the straw in the back of the barn. It was a hilarious but graphic retelling of the birth of Christ in a way that I am sure spoke powerfully to many people.

The Christmas crèche or nativity scene should take pride of place among our Christmas decorations, and the more vividly we can portray the Christmas story, the better! Evidently this tradition dates back to St. Francis of Assisi, who set up a stable scene in a cave not far from his home in Assisi as a way to demonstrate the Christmas story to people who could not read. He used real animals and people. As villagers gathered to see what he was doing, he told them about Jesus' birth in a stable and how angels appeared to shepherds telling them to go and find the Messiah who had been born.[18]

Latino families still enact the Christmas story as a community play called the Posada, which you may like to adapt for your family and church community. In the last weeks of Advent, the figures of Joseph and Mary from the parish crèche are moved from house to house. Each family has the figures for a day and puts them in a special place with a candle burning nearby. At the end of each day the family brings the crèche figures to the next family until they arrive at the church on Christmas Eve.[19]

The Shalom Community in Browns Summit, North Carolina, recaptured the magi theme as the focus for their celebration, which they called "Going to Find Jesus." They set up half a dozen stations around the house with a character from the Old Testament (Moses, David, Elijah, etc.), another from the first century (Pharisee, Sadducee, Samaritan, etc.), and another from contemporary culture at each station. The community members are pilgrims who stop and talk to each character and ask directions. They then invite the characters to join them. Finally, they reach the manger scene where some of the community's children are playing Mary and Joseph.[20] Of course a celebration like this needs lots of preparation, but it can provide exciting opportunities for your children to focus on the real meaning of Christmas. The characters have to be researched and scripted in pre-celebration studies. Gifts for Jesus need to be created and offered. Different family members could make these gifts and perhaps give them afterward to lonely people or a local nursing home.

Joining a Worldwide Celebration

We can draw from a rich variety of traditions as we seek to shape our own Christmas celebrations. Collecting ideas from other cultures or from traditions of the past may help your kids look beyond Santa Claus and the commercial hype. I suggest that you research your own family and cultural history and find out what observances your parents and grandparents used as children. Look at your church denomination's traditions, and think about ways that these could be incorporated into your observances. Researching the rich liturgical traditions of Catholic, Episcopal, Lutheran, and other denominations can provide tremendous inspiration for your worship and celebration.

For me Christmas will always engender memories of an Australian summer's feast with cold turkey and ham accompanied by an array of salads and fresh cherries. A trip to the beach was an added delight if the weather was particularly hot. And every Australian child knows that when Santa Claus reaches Australia, he swaps his reindeer for six white kangaroos—not a very Christ-centered idea, I know. At least in that land of 150 million sheep, we could easily identify with the shepherds as they listened to the angelic hosts announcing the birth of Christ!

Listen to the Beat—The Rhythm of Christmas

Fun, food, and festivity still have the power to transform our lives and show us the richness and wonders of our faith.

---

1. How could you prepare for the coming of Christ this Advent season?
   a. Write down one idea for spiritual preparation in your own life that you would like to commit to this coming Advent season.
   b. Write down one idea that would help your family better prepare for the coming of Christ this Advent season.
2. How could you make your Christmas celebration more Christ centered this year?
   a. Write down one suggestion you could incorporate in your celebrations to focus more intentionally on the love, joy, and peace Christ brings into the world.
   b. Write down one suggestion for your family celebrations that would focus on Christ's coming.

9

EASTER: THE RHYTHM OF HEALING

*T*he fragrant aroma of lamb impregnated with rosemary and garlic wafted toward me as I walked along the dusty street in Elevesis, Greece. Everywhere I looked men laughed and joked together as they squatted over barbecue pits erected in backyards and along the footpaths. They patiently turned the homemade spits, basting the lamb trussed firmly in place over the fire. This was Easter Sunday morning, and they were preparing for the most important feast of the year, the celebration of Easter and the resurrection of Christ.

The little blue-and-white houses bulged at the seams as family members gathered from all over the country to join the festivities. Inside, the women bustled around, preparing mountains of Greek salad with fresh feta cheese, sun-ripened tomatoes, and black Kalamata olives. Delicious herb-covered potatoes roasted in the ovens and sweet Greek pastries dripping with honey adorned enormous platters.

"Ella, ella!" (Come, come!) people called as we stopped to savor the smells. They beckoned us with wide welcoming smiles. Their hospitality reminded us that Christ welcomes all of us into God's family. We sat around the magnificent feast and participated in the joyous celebration.

Someone shouted, *"Christo anasti!"* (Christ is risen!)

We all answered, *"Allythos anasti!"* (He is risen indeed!) For the first time in my life, I felt as though I wasn't just reading the Easter story, I was living it.

The Easter Cycle—God's Rhythm for Healing

For most evangelical Christians, the celebration of Easter conjures up images of Easter Sunday feasts, an empty cross, and the celebration of Christ's resurrection. Just as the season of Christmas is far more than a day to commemorate Christ's birth, so Easter is far more than a day to celebrate the resurrection. Of course Easter brings the promise of eternal resurrection and the triumphant reminder that God's desire *is* for all to be healed and made whole. That is not only the glorious shout of Easter Sunday but also the central message of the entire biblical story.

Our walk with Jesus through the Easter season, however, also reminds us that Christ's resurrection was preceded by suffering and crucifixion. We will never fully appreciate the healing and redemptive power of the resurrection unless we also willingly face and identify with the cross—the agony and the suffering Christ endured to bring us healing. We can't just look at the cross and see it empty. We need to see Christ hanging on it for us.

In the church calendar, the cycle of Easter begins six and a half weeks before Easter Sunday with the season of Lent, a time for reflection and self-examination. The Easter cycle embraces the agonies of Jesus' walk toward Jerusalem, the horrors of Good Friday, and the crucifixion as well as the joys of Easter Sunday and the resurrection. It extends to Pentecost, the coming of the Holy Spirit, and the empowering of the church for service.

Like no other season of the church year, Easter invites us to enter with Jesus into the horrors and suffering of our lives and the world. We are not masochists who want to suffer. We are realists. As we enter into the Easter story, we identify with the One who was willing to endure crucifixion to offer us the hope of resurrection in the midst of our agonies and pain. By walking through Lent, Easter, and Pentecost, we enter into the life of the One who is present in every scene of suffering and agony in our world, the One who not only endures our suffering but also invites us to bear that suffering for others and so to offer them the hope of resurrection through him. In so doing we move closer to that health and wholeness we all crave for ourselves and for our world.

A Word about Suffering

When I was a young doctor in New Zealand, I struggled to find the proper view of suffering. I attended a Pentecostal church that was focused on Christ's power to heal. There was little thought of the suffering Christ endured to make this possible. People didn't seem to know how to cope with sickness, and those with chronic illnesses were often ignored or even ostracized. The possibility that God might expect us to share the suffering and pain of others was a totally foreign idea that made us extremely uncomfortable. Not surprisingly, Good Friday services reflected this. They could easily have been confused with an Easter Sunday celebration.

Later, as I worked with the poor and dying in the refugee camps in Thailand and in the villages of Africa, I was forced to question the assumption that God would remove all earthly pain. Even in my general practice, I often had to deal with the aftermath when someone was prayed for but was not healed. I struggled as I watched patients weighed down by guilt because prayer did not provide relief from their illnesses. Some of them had thrown away heart medicine or insulin injections in faith believing that God would heal them. One woman came to me in agony because of severe arthritis and back pain. She was afraid to take painkillers because she thought it reflected a lack of faith. Another was accused of harboring bitterness and anger that caused her pain, and yet another felt condemned because she was told she didn't pray enough.

I struggled too as friends who prayed desperately for healing died or suffered in agony and pain. My friend Liz Ewanoski died in April 2000 from an aggressive malignant melanoma that resisted all chemotherapy and surgical inter-vention. It devastated her body and caused agonizing pain and paralysis before her death. Even as I write, my friend Kate, who was once a vivacious and talented Christian speaker, is dying by inches of multiple sclerosis. Her once vital body and mind are slowly succumbing to this terrible disease. For people like these and their loved ones, the cross and its ability to bring redemption and healing is obscured by the accusing fingers of Christian brothers and sisters who heap guilt, condemnation, and lack of understanding on top of the physical pain.

All of us, no matter how strong our faith, will someday suf-fer pain, disease, and death. As much as we like to run away from suffering, we are all called eventually to go through our own Good Friday experience with its agonies of pain and crucifixion. Don't get me wrong. I don't believe God wants us to suffer—otherwise Christ would not have died for our sins. What I do believe is that God wants to use the suffering we endure to further his purposes in us and our world.

There are at least two purposes to sufferings. First, God uses it to bring us to a recognition of our own brokenness. We can't find true health and wholeness unless we suffer pain and admit we need the healing and redemption Christ offers. The apostle Paul put it this way: "We also rejoice in our sufferings, because we know that suffering produces perseverance, perseverance, character; and character, hope. And hope does not disappoint us, because God has poured out his love into our hearts by the Holy Spirit, whom he has given us" (Rom. 5:3–5).

In his book *God, Medicine, and Miracles*, physician Dan Fountain suggests that with any illness—and I would add with any other form of suffering or turmoil—we need to stop and ask God not *why* we are sick but *what* the illness can teach us about our lives, our relationships, and even our faith. Sometimes God uses illness to chastise us or to redirect us onto a better path. "In a real sense, an illness is an event with a voice. It is a teacher. Seeking healing and recovery is normal and very important. Seeking wisdom is even better."[1]

Suffering with Christ

The second purpose of suffering is to help us identify with the sufferings of Christ. In the early church the expectation of health and wholeness was closely linked to an acceptance of suffering as an identification with the sufferings of Christ. Physical illness was understood to be part of a larger paradigm in which God's grace works through human weakness. Christ calls us to identify with his suffering on the cross and to voluntarily enter into that suffering as we "carry each other's burdens" (Gal. 6:2a). When we come alongside those who suffer from illness, hunger, injustice, or any other trouble, we "fulfill the law of Christ" (Gal. 6:2b).

Often the suffering of others poses greater challenges to faith than our own suffering. As pastor and author Brian McLaren says, "But when we leverage ourselves into the situation in the right way, even the suffering of others can open for us experiences of God, especially as we are taken up into being part of the solution to their suffering. In our anger or frustration, we may pray, 'God, why do you allow this? Why don't you do something?' And at that moment, God has every reason to say something like this to us: 'I *have* done something: I've placed you in the situation with a compassionate heart and the ability to help. Now you can become an expression of my concern.'"[2]

According to Nouwen, McNeill, and Morrison in their book *Compassion: A Reflection on the Christian Life,* compassion comes from two Latin words, which together mean "to suffer with." They say, "Compassion asks us to go where it hurts, to enter into places of pain, to share in brokenness, fear, confusion and anguish. Compassion challenges us to cry out with those in misery, to mourn with those who are lonely, to weep with those in tears. Compassion requires us to be weak with the weak, vulnerable with the vulnerable and powerless with the powerless. Compassion means full emersion in the condition of being human."[3]

No wonder Paul encourages us to enter into the sufferings of others. "I want to know Christ and the power of his resurrection and the fellowship of sharing in his sufferings, becoming like him in his death, and so, somehow, to attain to the resurrection from the dead" (Phil. 3:10–11). By sharing in the suffering of others we also share in Christ's suffering and move through crucifixion toward the healing balm of resurrection. As Francis McNutt, a Catholic authority on healing, explains, "Through the power of the resurrection, God's life is breaking into our wounded world, and he gives us the power to cooperate with him by healing and reconciling man and all of creation."[4] How can we refuse to enter into the pain of others when we know that by so doing we actually cooperate with God in healing our broken world?

From Death to Resurrection

I have always been fascinated by the art of healing, and I believe God wants to see each of us healed from the physical, emotional, and spiritual illnesses that so bedevil and incapacitate us. The problem is that I, like most of us, have come to view modern medicine, not God, as the pathway to healing. When I see someone who is ill, I am more likely to reach for a prescription pad and an antibiotic than I am to pray and seek God's pathway for their healing.

On the other hand, I have seen people healed miraculously. I have watched cancerous tumors disappear and withered limbs straighten after a few simple words of prayer or after a patient was anointed with oil. On one occasion I received a phone call from an excited friend on a mission trip in Guatemala City. The previous evening at an evangelistic crusade, Maria, a young woman with a withered arm, had approached my friend Louise and begged for prayer. "She looked so helpless that I didn't want to disappoint her," Louise said. "To be honest, I didn't really expect anything to happen." But as Louise embraced Maria and prayed, something remarkable *did* happen. Under Louise's hand Maria's arm began to change. Louise watched in shock as the withered muscles and bones grew and strengthened and became whole. Louise, that great woman of faith and prayer, fainted on the spot!

I have not fainted on the rare occasions that I have seen miraculous cures, but I have responded with astonishment and awe. Yet why am I astonished? After all, the healing power of God is all around us. It is wonderfully woven into our bodies and into our world. The greatest miracle of all is not that we occasionally see people healed instantaneously but that most of us recover without miraculous intervention from our illnesses. When we cut ourselves or break a bone, the tissues heal—not because of medical treatment, which at its best only facilitates the body's innate ability to restore itself, but because of the miraculous system of cellular repair that God has put within us. When we catch a cold or the flu, our immune system jumps into action. God designed it that way. Even our emotional traumas can be defused by the mind's ability to process and heal painful events.

The most powerful symbol of healing in the Bible is the cross of Christ. In fact, it is the most powerful symbol of healing the world has ever known. Christ's power to redeem and transform through the cross brings healing to our bodies and to our souls and spirits. His power brings reconciliation in relationships that heals families and communities. Ultimately Christ's power will even bring healing and restoration to our broken world.

We cannot truly be made whole or really understand what it means to be healthy unless we deal with the problem of sin. We may get relief from a particular ailment or conflict, but we will never have real health of body, soul, and spirit unless we receive the restoration God made possible only through repentance and belief in Jesus Christ.

Healing and Salvation

Interestingly, the Greek word *sozo*, most commonly translated "save" in the New Testament, is also sometimes translated "heal." It means to heal, preserve, save, to be made whole. Missiologist David Bosch says it this way: "There is, in Jesus' ministry, no tension between saving from sin and saving from physical ailment, between the spiritual and the social."⁵ In the biblical sense, healing is *inseparable* from salvation because salvation is the process whereby a person is restored to the wholeness of being truly human—a person who is whole in body, mind, soul, and spirit, and living in right relationship with God as an individual, part of a community, and with God's good creation.

One of my privileges and my joys has been participating with God in bringing wholeness into people's lives. Maria was one of the first people I met with a cleft lip. Her pretty face was distorted by a gaping hole extending from her mouth to her nose, and her teeth protruded through this hole. Her hair was lank and unwashed, and her dress looked like a potato sack. She was so ashamed that she never left the house. She had no friends and no hope of marriage—a terrible calamity for a fourteen-year-old girl in the small Mexican village in which her family lived.

When team members from the *Anastasis* came to her village, they encouraged Maria to come to the ship for an operation. I will never forget how the surgery transformed her life. She appeared on board the ship several weeks after her surgery with a glowing face, marked only by a thin scar from mouth to nose. She wore a beautiful dress and long dangly earrings. Her hair was neatly trimmed and freshly styled. With delight she informed us that she was engaged to be married. It wasn't only her life that was transformed. After her operation she returned home to tell the villagers about a God who cared so much for her that he brought people literally from around the world to transform her face. Numerous villagers also professed faith in Christ.

How do we find the pathway to healing offered by God? Obviously our journey begins when we accept Christ as our

Lord and Savior. Our healing doesn't stop there, however, otherwise Christians would never be ill, suffer from emotional problems, or fall into sin. The unfolding of God's wholeness, the working out of our salvation, as Paul calls it (Phil. 2:12), is an ongoing process in which God slowly reveals more of our broken areas and brings us to the foot of the cross and to the Easter story time and time again. We need to celebrate not just Easter Sunday but the whole Easter cycle in the church calendar.

Lent—A Season for Self-Denial

The Easter cycle begins with the season of Lent, a forty-day fast that commemorates the time Jesus spent in the wilderness before starting his ministry. If you are good at mathematics you will realize that six and a half weeks is more than forty days. The early Christians never fasted on Sunday, which was always a mini celebration of the resurrection. I don't think Jesus enjoyed this kind of weekly reprieve however.

Lent is the deepest season of self-examination and self-denial in the church calendar. We are to prepare for the joy and feasting of Easter by giving ourselves an annual spiritual checkup. It is a time for self-denial and fasting as we recognize our need to be transformed. We invite God to crucify those things that keep us from giving our lives wholeheartedly to God. We deny ourselves by giving up some of the normal comforts of our lives. As our hearts become right with God we are free to celebrate Easter Sunday and experience the joy of the resurrection. A threefold discipline of prayer, fasting, and giving assists us in making the journey toward wholeness and joy: "Prayer . . . for the good of our souls, fasting for the good of our bodies, and almsgiving for the good of our neighbor."[6]

Lent begins with Ash Wednesday, a day that focuses on sin and death and our need to respond with repentance to God's redeeming love. In the early church this initiated a time of public penance for new Christians. They dressed in sackcloth and remained apart from social contact until they were reconciled with the Christian community on Maundy Thursday (the day before Good Friday).[7] That is a little radical for today. I can't imagine that our work colleagues would understand such a fashion, but at least we might like to attend an Ash Wednesday service where the pastor uses ashes to make a cross on the forehead of each worshiper as a sign of repentance.

Lent is traditionally a time to give up some of the comforts of life, but giving up is not meant to be the focus of Lent. Self-denial is not an end in itself. The real purpose of Lent is to free up time and resources through our self-denial so that we have more money and time to give to charity. Our self-denial is a way to enter into the fellowship of Christ's sufferings (Phil. 3:10) and identify more fully with those who are chronically hungry, oppressed, in pain, or in need of material goods we often take for granted.

The self-denial and self-examination of Lent provide a rhythm that enables us to let go of self-centeredness, materialism, and busyness (or anything else) that distract us from a wholehearted commitment to God. We literally nail them to the cross and reach out for the resurrection life that Christ offers—a life of caring, compassion, service, and closeness to God—the only life and rhythm that offers true health and wholeness. Lent is a time to develop rituals such as special prayers, Scripture readings, spiritual retreats, or involvement in a local or overseas mission that enables us to focus beyond ourselves and onto our responsibility to those who are hurting and in need.

The following prayer was developed for Mennonite congregations interested in liturgical renewal. I love to begin my morning devotions with this prayer during Lent. It has really helped me see myself as God does and has given me the courage to work on those areas in my life that still need to be transformed.

> In this Lenten season, O God, we come before you
> Asking you for courage to open our eyes.
> We want to see ourselves as you see us;
> The empty and barren places, the halfhearted struggles, the
>   faint stirrings of new life.
> We come, trusting your grace,
> Waiting for your illuminating word, longing for your heal-
>   ing light.
> Do not let us be blind to your presence
> Shine upon us, O God, and make our paths clear,
> For we pray in the name of Jesus, Amen.[8]

Spring-Cleaning for Lent

Interestingly the concept of spring-cleaning emerged from the practice of Lent. This was traditionally the time of year when one "cleaned house" first spiritually and then practically. "I think that spring house cleaning was an old way of introspecting," Gertrud Mueller Nelson says. "We clean house, inside and outside. We let in the fresh air, shake out the bedspreads, clean out the cupboards. We collect all the inner useless accumulations of our lifestyles and contribute them to the dust and ashes that we take up again on Ash Wednesday."[9] According to physician Herbert Benson, president of Mind/Body Medical Institute, focusing on repetitive motions like sweeping can help to lower blood pressure and heart rate. It also helps to bring the peace of mind needed to build our resilience to stress.[10] So maybe reintroducing spring-cleaning as part of our Lenten discipline would not be a bad idea!

There are many ways for families and church communities to participate in the spring-cleaning of Lent. What we "sweep out" or give up may be more than food. It could be soccer matches or TV or our social commitments. We could discuss with our families ways to give up our busyness and focus on the truly important things of God. Lent can be a trial run for a more focused and committed faith walk.

One suggestion you might like to discuss with your family is the possibility of taking a week or two of your annual vacation to go on a short-term mission trip during Lent. Arrange it to coincide with your children's Easter break so that you can experience this as a family. There is no better way to reevaluate our lives and struggles with the question of "How much is enough?" than to spend time with people who have far less than we do.

Lenten Pilgrimage

Just off the northeast coast of England, not far from the Scottish border, lies a tiny windswept island. It is surrounded by treacherous tidal sands, which the traveler can cross only at low tide by passing over a narrow causeway. As you pass in the train, you see a tiny fortress perched on top of the island's single hill in the treeless terrain. This is the Holy Island of Lindisfarne from which the Celtic monks spread the gospel throughout England and on into Europe during the fifth, sixth, and seventh centuries. Since then it has been a popular place for pilgrimages. Today, dedicated Christians walk many miles to reach the island, following the posts that have been placed along the safe route known as the Pilgrim's Way.

You might consider making your own pilgrimage to a holy Christian site in your neighborhood or overseas. If you don't have any holy sites near you, you may like to invent one like our friend David Pott did for a group of students in a discipleship-training program in London. Twelve students plus David walked from London to Canterbury in one week, a distance of about seventy miles. They imagined that Canterbury was the city of God and that they were Jesus and his disciples walking toward this holiest of cities in anticipation of that day when the promise of resurrection would be fully realized. As they walked they read and discussed the Scriptures. In the evenings while they massaged each other's feet and ministered to their blisters, they read John Bunyan's *Pilgrim's Progress*. For many it was the highlight of their training program.

Retreating from Distraction

Going on retreat, as already mentioned, is a practice that Tom and I instituted several years ago, and Lent is a prime time for one of our quarterly sessions. Many churches also traditionally hold their annual retreats during Lent. This may be a practice you want to consider. Retreating for forty days like Jesus did is a little much for most of us, but even a weekend away from the world's distractions can help us reevaluate our lives and priorities. There are many Protestant and Catholic retreat facilities available in most communities, or you may like to find an inexpensive cabin or motel in which to stay for the weekend.

Recently I came across *The Stress Detector Test* in *Oprah* magazine and decided to test my stress levels. Most of my life I have been a stressed-out workaholic. Much to my surprise, my score suggested that I was "either cheating, in denial or doing a great job of managing the stressful situations in my life."[11] As I thought about it, I realized that I manage stressful situations well these days. I am sure that the rhythm of retreating regularly is a major reason why. The self-examination of Lent has helped me become whole!

Food for Thought

One Lenten tradition you may want to introduce to your family is a guaranteed child pleaser: Eat pretzels each day. Evidently by the fifth century it was a tradition to eat little breads rolled and twisted to represent crossed arms over the chest as a visual reminder that Lent was a period of prayer and fasting. The breads were called "little arms" in Latin but later became known by the German translation "pretzel."[12] If you have time, make these with your children and put one at each person's place at the dinner table. Eating them at the end of each evening meal as you read the Scriptures together and pray is something that the whole family will come to love.

Palm Sunday and the Promise of Things to Come

One of my favorite church celebrations is Palm Sunday, which falls a week before Easter at the beginning of Holy Week. It commemorates Christ's triumphal entry into Jerusalem and foreshadows that wonderful homecoming event, Christ's glorious return at the end of the age. The imagery of Palm Sunday bursts with hope. As I think of the starving children I have worked with in Africa and Asia, see homeless people on the streets of Seattle, and hear my friends tell of their pains and emotional turmoil, I cannot help but think of that future day when God will make all things new and we will once more shout "Hosanna" at Christ's appearance. This imagery is most powerfully depicted in Isaiah's vision as Eugene Peterson translates it in *The Message:*

Pay close attention now:
  I'm creating new heavens and a new earth.
All the earlier troubles, chaos and pain
  are things of the past, to be forgotten.
Look ahead with joy.
  Anticipate what I am creating:
I'll create Jerusalem as sheer joy,
  create my people as pure delight.
I'll take joy in Jerusalem,
  take delight in my people:
No more sounds of weeping in the city,
  no cries of anguish;
No more babies dying in the cradle,
  or old people who don't enjoy a full lifetime;
One-hundred birthdays will be considered normal—
  anything less will seem like a cheat.
They'll build houses
  and move in.
They'll plant fields
  and eat what they grow.
No more building a house
  that some outsider takes over,
No more planting fields
  that some enemy confiscates,
For my people will be as long-lived as trees,
  my chosen ones will have satisfaction in their work.
They won't work and have nothing come of it,
  they won't have children snatched out from under
  them.
For they themselves are plantings blessed by GOD,
  with their children and grandchildren likewise GOD-
  blessed.
Before they call out, I'll answer.
  Before they've finished speaking I'll have heard.
Wolf and lamb will graze the same meadow,
  lion and ox eat straw from the same trough,
  but snakes—they'll get a diet of dirt!

Neither animal nor human will hurt or kill
anywhere on my Holy Mountain, says GOD.

Isaiah 65:17–25 MESSAGE

Our Episcopal church celebrates Palm Sunday in a fairly traditional fashion. The congregation gathers outside for a walk through the neighborhood. We bless the palm fronds and wave them in the air as we start our procession. We follow the cross bearer around the church and back into the sanctuary, singing "All glory, laud and honor to you Redeemer, King." As we sing my heart surges with hope and anticipation, longing for that day when Christ will enter our world with healing, wholeness, and the promise of redemption for all humankind.

You might like to be a little more adventurous. At Church Under the Bridge, which meets under a freeway viaduct in Waco, Texas, someone dressed as Christ rides in on a Harley Davidson motorbike. At another church in California, a live donkey leads the parade right into the sanctuary—though I am glad I don't have to clean up afterwards.

Trinity Lutheran Church in Lake Nebagamon, Wisconsin, devised a revision of the Palm Sunday story that was a tremendous hit with their children. The Sunday school made big palm trees out of old carpet rolls and put them in the aisle of the sanctuary. Two of the children dressed up as a donkey, one as the head and another as the tail. Jonathan, a disabled child in a wheelchair, played Jesus and led the donkey into the church. The tricky bit was getting the donkey to sit down at the appropriate time while the Sunday school sang a few songs. It was probably not the most liturgical start to the service, but even the older folks were enthusiastic and the message of Christ's triumphal entry into Jerusalem came through loud and clear.[13]

Foot Washing, Anyone?

My friend John hates the thought of someone else washing his feet. On one occasion when he could not avoid a foot-washing ceremony, he agonized for days over ways to cope. Eventually he decided that there was only one way to stop anyone touching his feet. He painted a brightly colored worm across the top of his toes and wriggled them furiously whenever someone approached. He managed to avoid every prospective foot washer! John would not do well at a Maundy Thursday or Holy Thursday service, which traditionally begins with communion and foot washing and follows with an all-night prayer vigil. It is a beautiful service. As Robert Webber says, "When we celebrate this service, we renew the covenant between God and ourselves and we are made ready for his death and resurrection."[14]

The Agony of Good Friday

No festival in the Christian calendar is more dramatic than the celebration of Easter with its incredible contrast between the pain and agony of Easter Friday and the joy and celebration of Resurrection Sunday. I love the Good Friday service when the sanctuary is somber and quiet, the altar is stripped of its vestments, and the cross is shrouded in black. The horror of Christ's crucifixion reaches deep into my soul. As we read Matthew 27:46 KJV, "My God, my God, why hast thou forsaken me?" I am often overwhelmed by the memories of times when I too have felt abandoned and alone. Knowing in that moment that Christ endured more pain and suffering than I can ever imagine powerfully opens a door in the midst of my darkness and provides a way for me to emerge into new life. After the service we leave the church in silence with the coldness of death echoing through our thoughts.

Growing up in Australia where Good Friday is a public holiday and attendance at church an expected tradition for most Christians, following Christ through this journey was never difficult. When I settled in the United States where most people work on Good Friday, I found it challenging. My willingness to enter into Christ's suffering took more discipline and suffering on my part too. There are creative ways we can become part of this somber event. For example, Susan takes a day off work every year and picks up her kids from school at noon so that they can all be ready for church in the evening. Barry takes an extended lunch break and attends a midday service at an Episcopal church near his office.

Mark Pierson, pastor of Cityside Baptist Church in downtown Auckland, New Zealand, started a tradition at his church several years ago that is now an annual event, attracting thousands of Christians and non-Christians. Local artists submit art around the theme of the stations of the cross—a traditional focus for Good Friday celebrations. Pieces of wood with nails hammered into them, sculptures of wire, papier-mâché and paint, and a magic Etch-A-Sketch screen of Jesus being laid in the tomb are but a few of the offerings that have depicted the pain of Christ's journey toward Calvary and the personal pain of many of the young artists. This idea has fired the imaginations of churches around the world. One church in Vancouver, British Columbia, enlisted their Sunday school children to produce art pieces. These have been a tremendous inspiration to the church congregation as well as to others in the community.[15]

The Joy of Easter Sunday

Easter Sunday is a totally different experience from the agony of Good Friday. For some the festivities begin with a Saturday night vigil and a midnight feast. For others the day begins with a sunrise service, a reminder of the women who came to the tomb at dawn, and a breakfast celebration. Traditionally, Easter Sunday is also a time for the baptism of new believers, who symbolically take on the story of Christ as they die to their sins and are raised to new life. At Tom Balke's Mennonite Brethren church in British Columbia, Easter Sunday and Good Friday services are an integrated whole. On Good Friday, each member is given a nail to hold throughout the service. At the appropriate moment they come forward and nail it into a life-sized cross. On Easter Sunday, chicken wire covers the cross and the nails, and people come forward to insert flowers into the wire. Tom says, "It is important that our nails are still there—the cross has not been sanitized."

Whatever your tradition, Easter is meant to be a time to celebrate with open arms and hearts as we rejoice in the wonder of the risen Christ and all that his sacrifice means to us and our world. It is a time for hospitality just as I experienced during that wonderful Greek celebration so many years ago. In some traditions the Easter table remains laden with food from Easter breakfast throughout the holiday season, ready for any guests who come. One of my dreams is to have a huge Easter barbecue when we roast a whole lamb, Greek style, over an open spit in the backyard and invite a crowd of people over for a huge celebration.

Easter Fun for the Family

Consider some of the many wonderful Easter traditions from other cultures as you search for meaningful rituals for yourself and your family. The Ukrainian custom of egg painting can be an inspiring experience that takes the focus away from commercialized Easter eggs. The egg is a symbol of new life and breaking through from imprisonment to freedom. We can decorate eggs with symbols of the resurrection and new life—spring flowers, butterflies, chickens, and rabbits as well as the joyful words "Alleluia" and "He is risen!" We can use these for an Easter egg hunt on Sunday morning. Of course you may need to get very creative with your meal planning if you don't want to waste all those hard-boiled eggs!

Martha Zimmerman suggests using plastic eggs filled with Scripture verses that tell the story of Christ's death and resurrection. Once the eggs have been collected they can be used as a visual aid in retelling the Easter story.[16] I know there are commercial versions of this idea available, but I think the creativity involved in putting your own eggs together is part of both the anticipation and joy of the experience.

Pentecost and the Coming of the Spirit

The day of Pentecost, fifty days after Easter, celebrates the coming of the Holy Spirit and the birth of the church. This festival draws us beyond the resurrection and into community with God's international family. It reminds us that through the Holy Spirit we are equipped and enabled to be God's servants in our needy world.

In medieval times Christians actually constructed Holy Ghost holes in church ceilings. As trumpets sounded a huge gold disc with a picture of a white dove painted on it was lowered into the sanctuary.[17] You may not want to do anything quite as radical as this at your church for Pentecost, but you can find creative ways to commemorate the day. In her entertaining book, *Scenes from Vicarage Life, Or the Joy of Sexagisma,* Catherine Fox suggests flying a kite since it taps into the wind-and-spirit imagery of the season.

In *Why Not Celebrate,* Sara Wenger Shenk suggests that Pentecost is a great time to hold a service for world peace. As the Holy Spirit fell on the early disciples, the barriers of language and culture were broken down and everyone heard what was being said in their native languages. We can use prayers in several languages or from different parts of the world to focus on our need for unity and cross-cultural understanding. If you plan a family celebration, perhaps your kids would like to dress in costumes from other cultures and make flags representing these countries. You can finish with a multicultural feast with dancing and food from different parts of the world. One great resource for such an event is *Extending the Table . . . A World Community Cookbook* by Joetta Handrich Schlabach. It has a wonderful array of recipes from around the world and recounts fascinating stories from the cultures associated with those recipes.

Listen to the Beat—The Celebration of Healing

In Australia and New Zealand, a constellation of stars called the Southern Cross lights the night sky. These stars also adorn our national flags. The stars of the Southern Cross are the first ones that children Down Under come to recognize. For hundreds of years these stars also guided sailors and travelers as they journeyed toward their destinations. Connecting to the true cross, the cross of Easter, as a regular rhythm of our lives reminds us that God's light directs us to the destinations he plans for us. His light has the ability to make us whole and to bring healing into every painful event of our lives.

In what ways would you like to connect more intentionally to the events of the Easter season?

1. *What is your greatest struggle in doing God's will? What is one Lenten discipline you could initiate to help you overcome this?*
2. *What is one thing you would like to do this coming Easter to connect more intentionally to the celebration of Christ's resurrection and redemption?*
3. *What is one ritual you would like to initiate around the celebration of Pentecost that would enable you to be better equipped to show God's love and redemption to others?*

10

RHYTHM FOR THE YEAR: MAKING THE ORDINARY EXTRAORDINARY

*T*he year 2002 marked the fiftieth year of Queen Elizabeth II's reign in England. It was celebrated throughout the British Commonwealth with jubilee parties, many of them street parties. Chris and Ali Lawrence and the members of the Round Chapel Neighbourhood Project situated in a poor and often violent community in London decided to host an alternative jubilee event—an event that harkened back to a far older understanding of Jubilee as expressed in Leviticus 25. They called it "reclaim the Jubilee."

Outside the Round Chapel, Lower Clapton Street was transformed from the media's image of "murder mile" into a majestic setting filled with flowers, music, storytelling, and food. Children, parents, and elderly people gathered to play games, dance, and eat a multicultural feast—a luxurious spread of meat and vegetables provided on a shoestring budget. Reggae, soul, and Cajun music reverberated through the street. Storytellers held the audience spellbound. At one point everyone paused for a moment's silence to remember those who had died on this stretch of road in acts of violence linked to drug dealing. At the same time, people recommitted themselves to working together for a more peaceful and just neighborhood. When the four hundred dinner guests reluctantly departed at 10 P.M. to the sounds of "Burn" (cow punk 1970s revival), their heads were filled with memories of laughter, multiple flavors, a myriad of colors, and many reflections on the true meaning of a strong community.

The Rhythm of Kingdomtide

The season of the church calendar after Pentecost is known as ordinary time, not because it is dull and boring, but because it does not have a distinct theme such as the birth, death, or resurrection of Christ. However, the creative use of feasting and fasting throughout this season does provide wonderful opportunities for us to connect the everyday events of our lives and cultures to our faith in extraordinary ways, as Chris and Ali and their community were able to do in Lower Clapton Street.

In chapter 2 we discussed the priorities that shaped Jesus' life and the lives of his followers throughout the centuries. We looked at the rhythm of spiritual practice, which gave rise to the daily pattern of prayer and the yearly cycle of feasts and fasts that have formed the main focus for this book. In

this last chapter, however, I want to focus on another priority
Jesus had that formed an essential pattern for much of his
life and those of his followers—the emphasis on community
with its rhythms of shared meals, hospitality, and service. I
believe these rhythms should be the focus for our celebrations
particularly during the six months after Pentecost.

The Rhythm of Community

The coming of the Holy Spirit at Pentecost drew Christ's
followers into a new community. They gathered together
regularly with the same enthusiasm for life that Jesus showed.
"They devoted themselves to the apostles' teaching and to
the fellowship, to the breaking of bread and to prayer. All
the believers were together and had everything in common.
Selling their possessions and goods, they gave to anyone as
he had need. Every day they continued to meet together
in the temple courts. They broke bread in their homes and
ate together with glad and sincere hearts, praising God and
enjoying the favor of all the people" (Acts 2:42, 44–47).

This extraordinary church family drew people from many
different cultures and social backgrounds. Rich and poor, male
and female, Jew and Greek lived together in community,
providing for each others' needs with joy and thanksgiving
as they remembered the hope they all shared in Christ—the
coming of a world in which all persons and all creation would
once more be made whole. Evidently it was not unusual
for women to round up destitute babies and orphans and
care for them. Christians in Egyptian cities even knocked
on poor people's doors and offered to move in to nurse the
sick, deliberately exposing themselves to illness.[1] They really
lived by the principle "love your neighbor as yourself" (Matt.
19:19).

In his letter to the Colossians, Paul described that first community coming together as a single caring body of believers. It's a good summary of why we need community today too.

> So, chosen by God for this new life of love, dress in the wardrobe God picked out for you: compassion, kindness, humility, quiet strength, discipline. Be even-tempered, content with second place, quick to forgive an offense. Forgive as quietly and completely as the Master forgave you. And regardless of what else you put on, wear love. It's your basic all-purpose garment. Never be without it. Let the peace of Christ keep you in tune with each other, in step with each other. None of this going off and doing your own thing. And cultivate thankfulness. Let the Word of Christ—the Message—have the run of the house. Give it plenty of room in your lives. Instruct and direct one another using good common sense. And sing, sing your hearts out to God! Let every detail in your lives—words, actions, whatever—be done in the name of the Master, Jesus, thanking God the Father every step of the way.
>
> Colossians 3:12–17 MESSAGE

I believe that the wholeness and well-being we all crave will never occur if all we work for is salvation in a small privatized spiritual compartment of our souls. Community is as essential today as it was two thousand years ago. Our faith is meant to draw us into a group of people who meet together on a regular basis, pray together, and work to see God's kingdom come on earth, albeit partially, in anticipation of that day when all things will be made new. Walter Brueggemann says: "If there is to be well-being, it will not be just for isolated, insulated individuals; it is rather security and prosperity granted to a whole community—young and old, rich and poor, powerful and dependent. Always we are in it together. Together we stand before God's blessings and together we receive the gift of life if we receive it at all. Shalom comes only to the inclusive, embracing community that excludes none."[2]

Whether we live together or only meet together regularly as a small group or church congregation isn't really the point. What matters is our willingness to enter into loving caring relationships with other believers who hold us accountable for the way we live. We must function in conjunction with a community of believers who support, encourage, and walk with us on our journey toward God and his purposes.

A Common Way of Life

There are many ways in which our involvement in community can enhance the rhythm of our lives. It gives us discipline, support and mentorship, and enables us to share Christ with others.

Sharing a common way of life with other likeminded believers can help us maintain the *discipline* we need to focus our activities on our faith rather than on the culture. This practice, called a rule of life, has formed the basis for community living throughout the history of Christianity. For some a rule of life involves the development of a complete set of guidelines for every part of life. A rule of life for others may be something as simple as a commitment by a group of friends to pray at the same time each day even if they are not able to be together in the same place. Use the internet to research options that are available, or take a retreat with a group of friends and work on a rule of life for yourself.

Probably the best-known and most enduring rule of all time is the Rule of St. Benedict, which has survived for fifteen hundred years and is credited with having saved Christian Europe from the ravages of the Dark Ages. This wonderful rule is still adhered to by numerous monastic and lay communities around the world. It has as much to say to twenty-first-century Christians as it did to sixth-century believers because it offers a way of life and an attitude of mind rather than a set of religious imperatives.

Benedict did not set out to found a religious order but merely compiled a "little Rule for beginners." "He wrote it for anyone who, renouncing his own will, should 'take up the strong and bright weapons of obedience in order to fight for the Lord Christ, our true King.'"[3] It is a fairly comprehensive rule that deals with the same issues we face in our world today—stewardship, relationships, authority, community, balance, work, simplicity, prayer, spirituality, and psychological development.[4]

In recent years a growing number of Protestant believers have discovered the richness that the Rule of St. Benedict can add to their lives. In *The Cloister Walk,* Kathleen Norris recounts some of her experiences in a monastic community and shares the down-to-earth nature of the Benedictine Rule, which has so much to offer busy people in need of spiritual rhythm. "Benedict knows that practicalities—the order and times for psalms to be read, care of tools, the amount and type of food and drink and clothing—are also spiritual concerns."[5] She says the Rule is especially helpful in relationships: "In a marriage, in a small town, in a monastery, it is all too easy to let things slide, to allow tensions to build until the only way they can be relieved is in an explosion that does more harm than good. Benedict's voice remains calm—persevere, bear one another's burdens, be patient with one another's infirmities of body or behavior. And when the 'thorns of contention' arise in daily life, daily forgive, and be willing to accept forgiveness."[6]

Listening to the Celts

The early Celtic Christians were also aware of the importance of this kind of community and the life rhythms it provided for their faith. According to George Hunter III, the establishment of Celtic monastic communities that drew lay people and clerics together into fellowship and shared spiritual practices was one of the reasons that the Celtic church spread as rapidly as it did throughout Ireland, Britain, and Europe. "The eastern monks often withdrew from the world into monasteries to save and cultivate their own souls; Celtic leaders often organized monastic communities to save other people's souls."[7]

Because of this difference they built communities in locations accessible to the traffic of the time. Though these communities included monks and nuns who lived disciplined ascetic lives, the groups were primarily populated by teachers, scholars, craftsmen, artists, farmers, and families. The lay people lived to the same rhythm as the monks and nuns. "The people supported each other, pulled together, prayed for each other, worked out their salvation together and lived out the Christian life together. Every person had multiple role models for living as a Christian."[8]

The Celtic style of monasticism has also gained considerable new adherents over the last few decades as many sincere people of faith search for communities that will support them, pray with them, and keep them accountable to God's call on their lives. One such group is the Community of Friends in Renewal established by Jane and Andrew Fitz-Gibbon in 1995 and based in Ithaca, New York. The community was deeply influenced by a number of historical Christian traditions including the Celtic, Anabaptist, and charismatic movements. It brings together evangelical, charismatic, and sacramental streams of the church. They see themselves as a "quasi-monastic" community whose rhythm of life flows out of a rule based around the daily office and the values and commitments they share as a community. There are no formal vows, but members are encouraged to live balanced lives of prayer, study, work, and rest.[9]

The 24-7 prayer movement also envisions a network of communities that harken back to the Celtic model. They have already established what they call "Boiler Rooms" in an old pub in Reading and Manchester, England. "These would be like Generation X monasteries where people pray, 24-7 continually throughout the year, ministering to the poor and producing all sorts of amazing new art and music as they glorify God," says Peter Greig, who heads up the international base of 24-7 prayer in England.[10] However, he also assured us that they are not into those funny hairdos that were so popular in the early monastic movement!

There is a burgeoning interest too in a more radical form of community, particularly among young people who want to live their faith with deep practical commitment. Several years ago Shane Claiborne, a zealous young man with long dreadlocks and patchwork homemade clothing, and a group of other students at Eastern College heard about some poor people in Philadelphia who were squatting in an abandoned church. The squatters were about to be evicted, so Shane and his friends joined them in the church in protest. His involvement with the poor radically changed the direction of Shane's life and resulted in the establishment of The Simple Way, a community with the purpose of living simply together with and among the poor in the inner city. This community seeks to model an incarnational presence among those at society's margins as they live with them, cry with them, laugh with them, and play with them. Shane told me that it is not unusual to return home to find that the sofa has disappeared because someone in the neighborhood needed it more than they did.[11]

The Supportive Community

In addition to giving us discipline, the Christian community enhances our spiritual growth through the provision of *sup-*

port and mentorship. We need others to hold us accountable for our spiritual development and to keep us focused on the call God has placed on our lives. It is impossible to follow Christ and his rhythms if we try to go it alone. We need friends who help us say no when we get too busy and who encourage us to go forward when we seek to establish new rhythms and goals. We need mature people of faith who help us identify and develop the gifts God has placed within us and who empower us to use those gifts in acts of service.

Matthew, a college student at Redeemer College in Canada, told me that he depends on his dorm friends, who really are his community at present, to help him get up early enough to have a regular prayer time in the morning. Matt is not a morning person. He often sleeps through his alarm clock. However, he has realized that early morning is the best time for him to spend time alone with God. Just before he goes to bed at night he e-mails one of his friends who loves getting up at the crack of dawn and tells her what time he wants to be woken in the morning. She bangs on his door until she is sure he is awake. This is a simplistic form of Christian community, but it helps us to understand how essential our friends and Christian mentors are in the development of our faith. In fact, the hardest adjustment many college students experience when settling into the workplace is the loss of community they experienced in college.

Finding a Soul Friend

Early Celtic Christians took seriously the need for mutual accountability. Each person developed a friendship with an *anamchara*, a "soul friend" with whom they could be vulnerable and accountable. This person was not a superior like a spiritual director, but rather a peer who both supported and challenged—a great idea that I think we would do well to use today.[12]

During a creativity seminar at Wabash Presbyterian Church in Auburn, Washington, participants decided to adapt this concept for their church. They suggested that each adult member be linked in a covenant partnership with a soul friend. Together they could work on mission statements and develop goals for the next three to five years that flowed out of that mission statement and provided a spiritual focus and rhythm for their lives 24/7. Soul friends would meet monthly to help each other set realistic goals and develop strategies to accomplish these goals. They could also hold each other accountable for their daily and weekly spiritual disciplines. Once a year the whole church could come together at a retreat for reflection, teaching, and the setting of common goals for the church's outreach into the community.

Even our children can be enlisted in this type of friendship to enhance their involvement in Christian service. Gerry and Carey wanted their home to be a place that would provide hospitality and community for others. When they moved into a new house recently, they decided it would be an open home for any who needed a place to stay. Eddie arrived from Haiti even before their boxes were unpacked. Since the unpacking process took most of Carey and Gerry's time and energy, their ten-year-old son, Graham, took Eddie under his wing, becoming his English tutor and helping him settle into this new culture. Eddie constantly shares stories of his life in Haiti, and Graham's life has been greatly enriched by his "soul friend."

The Rhythm of Shared Meals

Probably the greatest advantage of Christian community is not its ability to enrich our lives, but rather its potential for enabling us to *enrich the lives of others*. We cannot give full expression to the all-inclusive love of God if we function as isolated insulated individuals. To truly love each other, we must do far more than just exchange "the peace" in our Sunday morning worship services. Darrell Gruder says, "The practice of baptism introduces persons into a radically new kind of social relationship, no longer isolated individuals, they have become brothers and sisters adopted into the body of Christ to live a communal life as a sign of God's reign in the midst of human history. Incorporation into Christ involves movement from the alienating independence of competitive and self-interested individualism to the affirming interdependence of a community grounded in the obedience and self-giving of Jesus Christ."[13]

The Celebration of Communion

We demonstrate God's all-inclusive love and enrich the lives of others by sharing meals and extending hospitality. Early believers often gathered around common meals, which isn't surprising as eating has always been a ritual of togetherness for families, friends, and community members. In fact, in many cultures the refusal to eat together is a sign of enmity or pride. For Christian communities, these shared meals usually revolved around the remembrance and celebration of the Lord's Supper and gave rise to what became known as love feasts.

The Lord's Supper is probably the most famous meal in history and the celebration of communion in which we remember this final meal Jesus shared with his disciples is the most beautiful and graphic expression of Christian community imaginable. This is the last opportunity Jesus has to communicate with his disciples before his crucifixion. Surprisingly, on this last evening on earth he isn't out there healing the sick or feeding the hungry. He is in a private room eating a meal with the community of people who had not just been his working companions but who had become his closest friends. The emphasis of the whole evening is relationship and celebration. The evening culminates in that greatest celebration of all, the sharing of the bread and wine, which symbolizes the coming together of all of God's people at that great and joyful feast when we will join in a new and wonderful relationship in the kingdom of God.

One reason Tom and I love to worship in an Episcopal church is because we celebrate the communion every week. As we share the bread and wine, we remember not only those across the world with whom we unite as members of the body of Christ but also those throughout the ages who have come together around this same ritual. Walter Brueggemann explains, "The Holy Communion is our supreme experience of all God's people coming together, not on our terms but on God's terms. It is our vision of unity being actualized. . . . At the table and in all our *shalom* we focus finally on him who is the embodiment of *shalom*."[14]

In his book *The Forever Feast*, Dr. Paul Brand tells the story of an Arabic Baptist Church in Israel that beautifully illustrates the community nature of this celebration.

When they come together, each member brings a handful of grains of wheat. It may be from one's own field, or from their personal supplies at home. As they enter the church, they each pour grains into a common pot. When all have come, and while the worship goes on, the pot is taken to the kitchen and somebody quickly grinds the wheat in a stone mill, mixes in water and salt, and kneads the flour into a loaf. It is put in to the already-heated oven and baked.

By the time the service is finished and the church moves into the celebration of the Lord's supper and the breaking of bread, the loaf is ready. As each member breaks off his own portion, he or she is sharing grains of flour from every member of the church. When asked why they do this, one member replied, "As individual seeds we are each alone and separate from each other. Only when we are broken into flour and baked together can we experience full fellowship."[15]

Celebrating with Love

There are many other ways apart from the traditional communion service to remember the Lord's Supper. Unfortunately, the love feasts that commemorated this event for the early church gradually lost their significance and were eventually abandoned. They were revived by the Moravian church in 1727 to celebrate the unity and equality of all believers.[16]

This kind of remembrance can still form focal points for celebrating during Kingdomtide. Youth with a Mission, the parent organization for Mercy Ships, still uses love feasts as a regular festive meal to celebrate the joy of being a part of God's international family. These meals, which I have celebrated with YWAM communities in Europe, Africa, the United States, and New Zealand, are cherished memories of my twelve years with Mercy Ships. Every Friday night in my early days on the *Anastasis,* we decked out the dining room with crisp white tablecloths and the best silverware. We placed candles on the tables, and the cooks prepared a festive meal, made even more special since our diet the rest of the week was often an uninspiring parade of rice and beans or bread with vegetable soup.

In later years this practice gave rise to what we called "highways and byways" banquets. Crew members went out onto the streets and invited everyone they met to the ship for dinner. As seaports are often close to the red light districts of major cities, this meant we often entertained a motley collection of prostitutes, transvestites, and drug addicts. Many of them were deeply touched by the love of people they met onboard. Some made professions of faith, and their lives were radically changed.

Welcoming the Stranger

The offer of hospitality through sharing meals and shelter has always been an important part of Christian community. According to Christine Pohl in her inspirational book *Making Room,* the tradition of hospitality was once the practice of welcoming strangers into one's home with the offer of food, shelter, and protection.[17] "For most of the history of the church, hospitality was understood to encompass physical, social and spiritual dimensions of human existence and relationships. It meant response to the physical needs of strangers for food, shelter, and protection, but also a recognition of their worth and common humanity. In almost every case, hospitality involved sharing meals: historically table fellowship was an important way of recognizing the equal value and dignity of persons."[18]

She goes on to explain that it is through hospitality that we are able to express the values that are central to God's kingdom: "Hospitality is *central* to the meaning of the gospel . . . a lens through which we can read and understand much of the gospel, and *a practice by which we can welcome Jesus himself"* (emphasis added).[19] It was viewed not as an onerous duty but rather as a response of love and gratitude for God's love and welcome to us.[20]

Hospitality with the Celts

The Celtic Christians believed that hospitality was meant to be a custom in their homes, and they believed it was a key into the kingdom of God. To offer hospitality opened the possibility that they might be entertaining angels or even receiving Christ into their midst and thus fulfilling the law of love. Celtic monks often placed their guesthouses on the choicest sites within their settlements. While the monks lived on bread and water, their guests were fed the best food and drink. Columba supposedly wrote two of the hymns commonly attributed to him while grinding oats to make bread for guests expected on Iona. The monastery at Derry is said to have provided a thousand meals a day, and Brigid, who presided at the monastery of Kildare, was continually churning butter and making bread for visitors.[21]

The following blessing is an ancient Celtic rune for hospitality that is still often heard in Ireland:

We saw a stranger yesterday
We put food in the eating place,
Drink in the drinking place
Music in the listening place,
And with the sacred name of the triune God
He blessed us and our house, our cattle and our dear ones.
As the lark says in her song:
Often, often, often goes the Christ in the stranger's guise.[22]

Evidently the Celtic saints also extended open hospitality to animals and birds. One ancient story recounts that Kevin of Glendalough, monk at a major monastic site in Ireland, was once engaged in a vigil with his arms outstretched like a cross. A blackbird landed on the palm of his hand and laid a clutch of eggs. Not wishing to disturb the bird or damage the eggs, the saint stood with his arms outstretched until the baby birds had hatched.[23] This may be a little radical for us, but at least we can consider ways in which we can make our environments more friendly to wildlife.

Welcoming Jesus into Our Homes

For most of us, extending hospitality may be as simple as inviting a neighbor over for dinner or asking someone home for lunch after church. For Marcy it opened a whole new way of life. When Marcy's youngest daughter left for college, she was depressed at the thought of being an empty nester. Then one day she read the verse "Do not forget to entertain strangers, for by so doing some people have entertained angels without knowing it" (Heb. 13:2), and it occurred to her that she could use her home as a place of hospitality to travelers. She redecorated the empty bedrooms and let local ministries know that she had space available for overnight guests. "It has opened up a wonderful new life for me," she said. "Over the last year I have entertained a pastor and his wife from Idaho, a singing team from New Zealand, and a missionary couple from Africa. Each time someone comes to stay, I imagine that Jesus is coming to visit. It has not only enriched my life, it has enriched my faith too."

Nadine, a hairstylist in Seattle, Washington, has expressed hospitality in a totally different way. She wants to be "God's love and healing hands to those I encounter" and believes that the best way she can extend God's hospitality to people is through her work. "I wanted to provide an environment in which my clients can relax, unwind, and feel unhurried," Nadine said. So she cut down on her number of appointments and greets clients with a cup of tea or coffee. Then she washes their hair, massages their scalp, and listens to their worries while she cuts their hair. This new focus has not necessarily made life easy for Nadine. "Taking more time for each client has meant a decrease in income," she explained. She had to simplify her life to break even, but the reward is worth it. "Watching the muscles relax and the frowns disappear is a real joy," Nadine said. Life has never been more satisfying.

Looking Back to the Old Testament Feasts

One of the greatest weapons we can utilize against the pressures and deceptive allure of the consumer culture is the Christian gift of *fun and celebration*. My husband and I often tell people that the best place to start developing a new rhythm is *not* in cutting back and *certainly not* in planning an all-night prayer meeting *but by planning a party*—and not just any old party, but a party that connects deliberately to the important events of our faith. There are many celebrations apart from Christmas and Easter that can provide opportunities to share meals with friends and strangers and help us connect to the rhythms of our faith. One possibility is to celebrate the Jewish feasts from the Old Testament. Feasting and festivity were always pivotal points in Judaism, and the Jewish calendar still provides a rich resource for celebration.

The entire Jewish year is a cycle of seasons and festivals, many of which date back to God's instructions to the children of Israel after their flight from Egypt. In *Celebrate the Feasts of the Old Testament in Your Own Home or Church*, Martha Zimmerman suggests that celebrating these Old Testament feasts is a wonderful way to connect our children to their biblical heritage. "If your child sees, hears, smells, tastes and feels the Word of God, profound impressions will be made in that young life! Celebrate and remember the deeds of the Lord as a family. Children learn what they live!"[24]

Martha gives helpful ideas for family celebrations at Passover, Omer, Shavuoth, Rosh Hashanah, Yom Kippur, and Sukkoth. The Jews had feasts and festivals for everything good and everything bad that happened in their history—a good reminder to us that we too need to remember the events of the past with celebration or somber remembrance where appropriate.

Birthdays, anniversaries, and rites of passage too can provide a focus for our hospitality. Even other more mundane events such as when school's out or children go back to school may be occasions that you want to consider reshaping with a faith focus. In *Why Not Celebrate!* Sara Wenger Shenk recounts the story of the Shufords, who plan a family gathering for one of the last evenings before school starts. They bake a cake adorned with the names of the children's schools and give each child a Scripture verse as their "watchword" for the new school year. During the evening everyone writes personal goals for the next year. These are sealed in envelopes that are opened six months later as a checkup time.

Even income tax time, which is one of my most difficult times of the year as I struggle to pull all our financial records together, can be transformed if we view it as an occasion to celebrate God's faithfulness over the past year. The day after you send in your tax return, plan a celebration with your family to thank God for the completion of this onerous task and for his abundant provision in the last twelve months. Get each family member to recount a story that demonstrates God's faithful provision for personal needs and for the needs of others through your generous giving. Read some Scripture, and finish with a petition for God's provision for the future.

Tax time is also a good time to evaluate your financial goals for the next twelve months based on God's economic values of generosity, mutual concern, and service. One appropriate Scripture to meditate on is 2 Corinthians 9:11: "You will be made rich in every way so that you can be generous on every occasion, and through us your generosity will result in thanksgiving to God."

We live in a culture in which we truly have been made rich in every way, and yet we are constantly barraged with messages that convince us we still don't have enough. We rarely take time to rejoice in God's provision, so we are often deprived of the joy of sharing God's bounty with others and of the blessing of a heart that is grateful toward God. As the writer of Proverbs reminds us, "A cheerful heart is good medicine" (Prov. 17:22a).

The Rhythm of Service

In addition to sharing meals and hospitality, we express God's all-inclusive love through the acts of service we perform in the community. Again we can go back to the New Testament for understanding. "This is how we've come to understand and experience love: Christ sacrificed his life for us. This is why we ought to live sacrificially for our fellow believers, and not just be out for ourselves. If you see some brother or sister in need and have the means to do something about it but turn a cold shoulder and do nothing, what happens to God's love? It disappears. And you made it disappear" (1 John 3:16–18 MESSAGE). The Scriptures are clear that our responsibility as Christians extends beyond our own needs to the community around us.

One creative idea that could provide a rhythm of service for your family came out of a seminar we held in Winnipeg, Manitoba. The suggestion was to plan the family's mission involvement and giving around the seasons of the year. The beginning of the school year can be a time to provide school lunches or boxes of educational materials for the underprivileged children in your area. Or you might give money to a mission organization that is involved in childhood education in Africa or Asia. There are 90 million girls of elementary age in the world who do not attend school. Connecting your family's giving to an awareness of disparities such as this will not only help your children become more generous but also raise their awareness of their own privilege.

Thanksgiving is a wonderful time to concentrate on gratitude for God's blessings and abundant provision. Why not think about getting your children involved in a local homeless shelter or offer hospitality to seniors or solo-parent families who have no other family members to help them? Christmas and Lent also provide many wonderful opportunities for hospitality to those less fortunate than ourselves.

Summer opens up a number of creative possibilities for community service. If you are a keen gardener like I am, the summer is a time to share your harvest with the poor. Perhaps you would like to join the thousands of gardeners who "plant a row for the hungry" and donate their produce to a local food bank. Alternatively you could involve your family in a project that makes them feel they are sharing the harvest of their education with others. Kids of ten and twelve often have more than enough computer skills to be able to tutor other children, or they may be able to teach kids to play basketball or football or soccer. One bonus of this is that their own skills often improve in the process. Sit down with your kids and discuss what skills they would like to share with others over the coming year. Do some research on organizations in your town that are open to your involvement.

Even our neighborhoods can provide opportunities to reach out with the love and caring heart of God. When two of Patty's neighbors, Chris and Jack, who used to be best friends had a disagreement, she enlisted her son Jake's help in bringing about reconciliation. She prayed regularly with Jake for their neighbors, asking, "How can we show the love of Christ to our neighbors today?" Jake hated the estrangement between Chris and Jack and came up with a strategy to bring them together again. He knew they once played basketball together, so he invited Chris over to play with him. The moment Chris arrived Jake headed off to get Jack, and by the end of the afternoon they had talked out their disagreement and the three of them were happily shooting hoops together.

Celebrate with Creativity

In her book *Walking on Water: Reflections on Faith and Art*, Madeleine L'Engle reminds us that all children are born artists endowed with rich unfettered imaginations. All our senses are in touch with *being* rather than doing. Unfortunately, she believes that as we grow we are corrupted by the "dirty devices of the secular world," where myth and fairy tale must be discarded.[25] The vivid purple clouds and yellow skies of childhood must give way to the *real world* where clouds are white and skies are blue. Madeleine goes on to say, "We write, we make music, we draw pictures, because we are listening for meaning, feeling for healing. And during the writing of the story, or the painting, or the composing or singing or playing, we are returned to that open creativity which was ours when we were children. We cannot be mature artists if we have lost the ability to believe which we had as children. An artist at work is in a condition of complete and total faith."[26]

In the celebration of our own creativity and in the appreciation of someone else's artistic or musical accomplishments, we often find both meaning and healing. Painting a picture, writing a poem, listening to music, or creating our own music, are all forms of celebration that enrich our lives and bring healing to our battered senses. Here too scientific research reinforces what many of us have known intuitively for years. Therapists are now using music and art as part of the treatment for a wide range of emotional and physical disorders.

The creative arts do more than just stimulate our senses, however. They are often the medium through which we find the inspiration to make our dreams for God's shalom kingdom real. In many ways they can make tangible the intangible and open the doorway to a new world—that hoped-for world in which all that God promises for the future comes into being. Whenever we draw a picture, write a poem, or compose a piece of music that focuses on God's shalom purposes for our lives and for the world, we give form and substance to our deepest longings and our biggest dreams. Human creativity that is attuned to God's purposes has power to transform and inspire as nothing else can.

"Nothing else comes close to art in giving voice to our deepest needs and helping us to move on into 'the new,'" states Andrew Rumsey in *Third Way* magazine. He goes on to say, "The more that human creativity is tuned to the note of Christ, the more it must become itself—if Christ is the genius of creation, art will discover its transformative power in relation to him."[27] Walter Brueggemann also recognizes the importance of artistic expression in focusing us on God's wonderful purposes for the future. He talks about poets as "discerners of newness, people who fashion images hoped for that have not yet become visible, who sense the deep undertow of life and welcome it."[28] Expressing our creativity through the eyes of our faith really does unleash in us the transforming power of God, and it does assist us in both controlling and making way for the changes that are impacting our lives.

One of the best ways to celebrate during this season of Kingdomtide is to hold a "creativity party." Encourage participants to bring paints, paper and pencils, or musical instruments. Choose a theme such as the kingdom of God as a banquet feast. Read some Scriptures like Luke 14:12–14 and Matthew 22:1–14 and spend some time meditating on these verses. Then ask people to paint pictures, write poetry, and compose songs. It is amazing to see how people come to life when invited to share their creativity in this way. In the process all of us are drawn closer to the God we serve and the kingdom we are anticipating.

Listen to the Beat—Making the Ordinary Extraordinary

In the early 1900s a lonely camel rider came through the vast expanse of the Australian outback dreaming an impossible dream for thousands of isolated people who inhabited the western two-thirds of this vast continent. In the days when telegraph wires were necessary for long-distance communication, he envisioned a network of wireless radios connecting every isolated settlement to towns where spiritual guidance and medical help was available. He dreamed of providing medical aid, communication, and mail service to people who were often out of touch for months at a time. People thought he was crazy because in the early 1900s the technology did not exist to transmit radio signals over hundreds of miles.

The man was Reverend John Flynn, now known as "Flynn of the Inland" because of the incredible work he did to bring help and healing to the inland of the continent. Out of his impossible dream came the founding of the Australia Inland Mission Nursing Services, the famous Royal Flying Doctor Service, and a simple foot-pedaled wireless radio that enabled even the most remote outback inhabitants to contact the outside world. His life was an inspiration to me and to many other young Australians.

John Flynn never regarded himself as a great or unusual person. He saw himself as an ordinary man whose life was in synch with an extraordinary God. This God, John Flynn believed, imparted dreams from heaven for men and women to bring into reality on earth.

I believe God has placed within all of us "impossible dreams" that we are called to bring into reality on earth—dreams that will bring glimpses of God's shalom world into people's lives. All of us have the potential to do extraordinary things, but like John Flynn we need to discover the joy of living as God intended—in synch with him and his shalom rhythms. Amazingly when we enter into this way of life, we *will* find the fullness and wholeness that God wants for us. We will see as E. Stanley Jones proclaims that "to be a Christian you may have to give up some things, but not to be a Christian you will have to give up everything—everything worthwhile. In giving up things for Christ I gave up nothing but what subtracted from me, and when I got Him I got everything that added to me."[29]

How could you take the ordinary things of your life and make them extraordinary?

1. *What involvement in community would provide you with support and mentorship so that you could live more intentionally to God's rhythm?*
2. *What is one way in which you could extend hospitality to others over the next three months?*
3. *What is one way that you could make Christian service a part of your yearly rhythm in the next year?*
4. *What is one new celebration that you would like to inaugurate for your family over the coming year?*

Notes

Introduction

1. Robert D. Putnam, *Bowling Alone: The Collapse and Revival of American Community* (New York: Simon & Schuster, 2000), 72.
2. E. Stanley Jones, *The Way* (New York: Abingdon-Cokesbury, 1936), 42.
3. S. E. Massengill, *A Sketch of Medicine and Pharmacy* (Bristol, Tenn.: S. E. Massengill, 1943), 16, quoted in S. I. McMillen, M.D., *None of These Diseases* (New York: Pyramid, 1967), 9.
4. For a comprehensive discussion of *shalom*, see Walter Brueggemann, *Living Toward a Vision: Biblical Reflections on Shalom* (New York: United Church Press, 1976).
5. Ibid., 16.
6. Richard Foster, *Freedom of Simplicity* (San Francisco: HarperCollins, 1984), 30.
7. James E. Metzler, "Shalom Is the Mission," in Robert L. Ramsyer, *Mission and Peace Witness* (Scottdale, Pa.: Herald, 1978), 40.
8. Catherine Rauch, "Probing the Power of Prayer," *CNN.com*, 13 February 2003, <http://www.cnn.com/2000/HEALTH/alternative/01/18/prayer.power.wmd/>.

Chapter 1 *Running for Your Life*

1. See James Gleick, *Chaos: Making a New Science* (New York: Penguin, 1987).
2. Brian Fagan, *The Little Ice Age* (New York: Basic, 2000), 23–78.

3. Donella Meadows, Dennis Meadows, and Jorgen Randers, *Beyond the Limits: Confronting Global Collapse, Envisioning a Sustainable Future* (White River Junction, Vt.: Chelsea Green, 1993), 15.

4. John De Graaf, David Wann, and Thomas H. Naylor, *Affluenza: The All-Consuming Epidemic* (San Francisco: Berrett-Koehler, 2001), 36.

5. Ibid., 44.

6. Jay Walljasper, "The Speed Trap," *Utne Reader,* March/April 1997, 42.

7. John Leland, with Christopher Dickey, Debra Rosenberg, and Steve Rhodes, "Taking Off, Tuning In," *Newsweek,* 27 July 1998, 47.

8. Robert D. Putnam, *Bowling Alone: The Collapse and Revival of American Community* (New York: Simon & Schuster, 2000), 72.

9. George Ritzer, *Enchanting a Disenchanted World: Revolutionizing the Means of Consumption* (Thousand Oaks, Calif.: Pine Forge Press, 1999), 8–9.

10. *Ship of Fools.com: The Magazine of Christian Unrest* <http://www.ship-of-fools.com/Gadgets>.

11. Ibid.

12. Patricia Leigh Brown, "Megachurches as Minitowns," *New York Times,* 9 May 2002, D6.

13. Ibid., D1.

14. Don Tapscott, "The Hype Behind the Hypernet," *Enroute,* March 2002, 25.

Chapter 2 *Do You Hear the Beat?*

1. Carolyn Rance, "Managers Are Here to Help," *Melbourne Age,* 3 July 1999, F1.

2. Alexander Stille, "Slow Food's Pleasure Principles," *Utne Reader,* May/June 2002, 56.

3. Ibid., 58.

4. Francine Klagsbrun, *Jewish Days: A Book of Jewish Life and Culture* (New York: Farrar Straus Giroux, 1996), 1.

5. E. Stanley Jones, *The Way* (New York: Abingdon-Cokesbury, 1946), 6.

6. Ibid., 4.

7. Ibid., 31.

8. Ibid., 51.

9. N. T. Wright, *The Original Jesus: The Life and Vision of a Revolutionary* (Grand Rapids: Eerdmans, 1996), 83.

10. Christine and Tom Sine, *Living on Purpose: Finding God's Best for Your Life* (Grand Rapids: Baker, 2002), 49.

11. For a comprehensive look at how to develop a mission statement and use it to set goals for your life, see ibid., 78–87.

12. Richard Foster, *The Celebration of Discipline* (San Francisco: Harper & Row, 1978), 30.

13. Lesslie Newbigin, *The Open Secret* (Grand Rapids, Eerdmans, 1995), 52.

14. N. T. Wright, *The Challenge of Jesus* (Downers Grove, Ill.: InterVarsity, 1999), 43.

15. Howard Snyder, *The Community of the King* (Downers Grove, Ill.: Inter-Varsity, 1977), 74.

16. Miroslav Volf, *Work in the Spirit: Toward a Theology of Work* (Oxford: Oxford University Press, 1991), 84.

17. Pamela Paul, "Time Out," *American Demographics,* June 2002, 34–41.

18. John Christoffersen, "High Schoolers Encouraged to Take 40 Winks," *Burbank (Calif.) Daily News,* 10 November 2002.

19. "Looking for the Sandman," *Berkeley Wellness Letter,* University of California, Berkeley, Calif., vol. 15 (April 1999): 5.

20. Rodney Clapp, *A Peculiar People: The Church as Culture in a Post-Christian Society* (Downers Grove, Ill.: InterVarsity, 1996), 88.

21. David Bosch, *Transforming Mission* (Maryknoll, N.Y.: Orbis, 1991), 48.

22. Brother Victor-Antoine d'Avila-Latourrette, *A Monastic Year: Reflections from a Monastery* (Dallas: Taylor, 1996), 37.

23. Esther de Waal, *The Celtic Way of Prayer: The Recovery of the Religious Imagination* (New York: Doubleday, 1997), 53.

Chapter 3 *Practice Makes Perfect*

1. Fredrica Mathewes-Green, "Death to the World: Punks Turned Monks," *The Ooze: Conversation for the Journey,* <http://www.theooze.com/articles/article.cfm?id=150&page=1> (13 February 2003).

2. Ibid.

3. Ellis Peters, *A Morbid Taste for Bones* (New York: Mysterious, 1977).

4. Sara Wenger Shenk, *Why Not Celebrate!* (Intercourse, Pa.: Good Books, 1987), 17.

5. Martha Beck, "Creating Special Moments that Enhance and Enrich Your Life," *Real Simple,* April 2000, 192.

6. Rodney Clapp, *A Peculiar People: The Church as Culture in a Post-Christian Society* (Downers Grove, Ill.: InterVarsity, 1996), 119.

7. Gertrud Mueller Nelson, *To Dance with God: Family Ritual and Community Celebration* (Mahwah, N.J.: Paulist, 1986), 11.

8. Ibid., 12.

9. Herbert Anderson and Edward Foley, *Mighty Stories, Dangerous Rituals* (San Francisco: Jossey-Bass, 1998), 22.

10. Nelson, *To Dance with God,* 25.

11. Richard Foster, *Prayer: Finding the Heart's True Home* (San Francisco: HarperSanFrancisco, 1992), 105.

12. Paul Hiebert, *Anthropological Reflections on Missiological Issues* (Grand Rapids: Baker, 1994), 167.

13. Beck, "Creating Special Moments," 194.

14. M. Robert Mulholland Jr., *Invitation to a Journey* (Downers Grove, Ill.: InterVarsity, 1993), 59–60.

15. Henry Morgan, ed., *Approaches to Prayer: A Resource Book for Groups and Individuals* (Harrisburg, Pa.: Morehouse, 1991).

16. Esther de Waal, *Every Earthly Blessing* (Ann Arbor, Mich.: Servant, 1991), 10–11.

17. Esther de Waal, *The Celtic Way of Prayer: The Recovery of the Religious Imagination* (New York: Doubleday, 1997), 61.

18. Douglas Hyde, "Religious Songs of Connacht" (Dublin: Irish University Press, 1906), in de Waal, *Celtic Way of Prayer*, 78.

19. William John Fitzgerald, *Blessings for the Fast Paced and Cyberspaced* (Leavenworth, Kans.: Forest of Peace Publishing, 2000), 220.

20. See *The Northwest Yearly Meeting Statement: Faith and Practice*, July 2000, <http:/nwfriends.org/FandP/fandp4.html>.

21. Terry Wallace, *Quaker Life*, Jan/Feb 2001, 10.

Chapter 4 *Catch the Rhythm*

1. Luci Tumas, "What a Difference the Word Makes!" *In Other Words* (a Wycliffe publication), August 2002.

2. Madeleine L'Engle, *Walking on Water* (Wheaton: Shaw, 1980), 181.

3. Kathleen Norris, *The Cloister Walk* (New York: Riverhead, 1996).

4. *Celtic Daily Prayer: Prayers and Readings from the Northumbria Community* (San Francisco: HarperSanFrancisco, 2002).

5. Paul Hiebert, *Anthropological Reflections on Missiological Issues* (Grand Rapids: Baker, 1994), 168.

6. Ibid., 169.

7. Dennis Linn, Sheila Fabricant Linn, and Matthew Linn, *Sleeping with Bread: Holding What Gives You Life* (Mahwah, N.Y.: Paulist, 1995), 1.

8. Debbie Trafton O'Neal, *Thank You for This Food* (Minneapolis: Augsburg Fortress, 1994), 13.

9. Janet Kagan, *Hellspark* (New York: Tor, 1988), 219.

10. Patricia Leigh Brown, "Cinematography and Chilling Out? That's Scouting," *New York Times*, 13 May 2002, A9.

11. Herbert Anderson and Edward Foley, *Mighty Stories, Dangerous Rituals* (San Francisco: Jossey-Bass, 1998), 49.

12. William John Fitzgerald, *Blessings for the Fast Paced and Cyberspaced* (Leavenworth, Kans.: Forest of Peace Publishing, 2000), 21.

13. Christine Aroney-Sine, *Tales of a Seasick Doctor* (Grand Rapids: Zondervan, 1996).

14. Tom Sine, *Mustard Seed vs McWorld* (Grand Rapids: Baker, 1999), 41.

15. Brother Victor-Antoine d'Avila-Latourrette, *A Monastic Year: Reflections from a Monastery* (Dallas: Taylor, 1996), 81.

Chapter 5 *Prescription for a Healthy Life*

1. For a more detailed account of this story, see Christine Aroney-Sine, *Tales of a Seasick Doctor* (Grand Rapids: Zondervan, 1996), 48–49.

2. M. Basil Pennington, *Centering Prayer: Renewing an Ancient Christian Prayer Form* (Garden City, N.Y.: Image, 1982), 29.

3. Henri Nouwen, "Letting Go of All Things," *Sojourners,* May 1979, 6.

4. Pennington, *Centering Prayer,* 22.

5. Richard Foster, *Prayer: Finding the Heart's True Home* (San Francisco: HarperSanFrancisco, 1992), 3.

6. James Mulholland, *Praying Like Jesus* (San Francisco: HarperSanFrancisco, 2001), 34.

7. E. Stanley Jones, *The Way* (New York: Abingdon-Cokesbury, 1946), 197.

8. Henri Nouwen, Donald McNeill, and Douglas Morrison, *Compassion: A Reflection on the Christian Life* (New York: Image, 1983), 134.

9. Jan Johnson, *When the Soul Listens* (Colorado Springs: NavPress, 1999), 38.

10. 24–7 Prayer <http://www.24-7prayer.com>.

11. For more information on the 24-7 prayer network, visit their web site at http://www.24-7prayer.com.

12. Foster, *Prayer,* 13.

13. Ibid., 15.

14. Oswald Chambers, *My Utmost for His Highest* (New York: Dodd, Mead & Company, 1935), 44.

15. Johnson, *When the Soul Listens,* 43.

16. Jo Kadlecek, *Feast of Life* (Grand Rapids: Baker, 1999), 35.

17. Steve Adams, "Ancient Modern Ministry," *Youthwork,* January 2002, 21.

18. Ibid., 23.

19. Clifford E. Bajema, *At One with Jesus* (Grand Rapids: CRC, 1998), 5.

20. Ibid., 7.

21. Richard Foster, *The Celebration of Discipline* (San Francisco: Harper & Row, 1978), 15.

22. Bajema, *At One with Jesus,* 8.

Chapter 6 *Rhythm for the Day*

1. *Ship of Fools.com: The Magazine of Christian Unrest* <http://www.ship-of-fools.com/gadgets>.

2. Wayne Muller, *Sabbath: Finding Rest, Renewal and Delight in Our Busy Lives* (New York: Bantam, 1999), 71.

3. Richard Foster, *Prayer: Finding the Heart's True Home* (San Francisco: HarperSanFrancisco, 1992), 13–14.

4. Dorothy C. Bass, *Receiving the Day: Christian Practices for Opening the Gift of Time* (San Francisco: Jossey-Bass, 2000), 17.

5. Dennis Linn, Sheila Fabricant Linn, and Matthew Linn, *Sleeping with Bread: Holding What Gives You Life* (Mahwah, N.Y.: Paulist, 1995), 17.

6. For a comprehensive look at how to develop a biblically shaped mission statement in order to reinvent your life with a kingdom focus, see Christine and Tom Sine, *Living on Purpose: Finding God's Best for Your Life* (Grand Rapids: Baker, 2002).

7. Esther de Waal, *The Celtic Way of Prayer: The Recovery of the Religious Imagination* (New York: Doubleday, 1997), 52.

8. Sara Wenger Shenk, *Why Not Celebrate!* (Intercourse, Pa.: Good Books, 1987), 18.

9. David Adam, *The Rhythm of Life: Celtic Daily Prayer* (Harrisburg, Pa.: Morehouse, 1996), 1.

10. Ibid., 2.

11. William John Fitzgerald, *Blessings for the Fast Paced and Cyberspaced* (Leavenworth, Kans.: Forest of Peace Publishing, 2000), 190.

12. David Robinson, *The Family Cloister* (New York: Crossroads, 2000), 67–68.

13. See "Gadgets for God," *Ship of Fools.com*, <http://www.ship-of-fools.com/gadgets/index.html>.

Chapter 7 *The Sabbath Rest*

1. Francine Klagsbrun, *Jewish Days: A Book of Jewish Life and Culture* (New York: Farrar, Straus, and Giroux, 1996), 9.

2. Ibid., 15.

3. Ibid., 11–13.

4. Wayne Muller, *Sabbath: Restoring the Sacred Rhythm of Rest* (New York: Bantam, 1999), in Stephen Caldwell, "Working on Kingdom Theology," *The Life@Work Journal* 4 (1): 4.

5. Abraham Joshua Heschel, *The Sabbath* (New York: Farrar, Straus, and Giroux, 1951), 22.

6. Genesis rabba 10, 9, in ibid, 23.

7. Heschel, *The Sabbath*, 74.

8. David Chidester, *Christianity: A Global History* (San Francisco: HarperSanFrancisco, 2000), 61.

9. R. Paul Stevens, *Seven Days of Faith: Every Day Alive With God* (Colorado Springs: NavPress, 2001), 221.

10. Ibid., 215.

11. Ibid., 220.

12. Tilden Edwards, *Sabbath Time: Understanding and Practice for Contemporary Christians* (New York: Seabury, 1982).

13. *Celtic Daily Prayer: Prayers and Readings from the Northumbria Community* (San Francisco: HarperSanFrancisco, 2002), 87.

14. Marc Gunther, "God & Business," *Fortune*, 9 July 2001, downloaded from <http://www.fortune.com> (9 July 2001).

15. Marva Dawn, *Keeping the Sabbath Wholly* (Grand Rapids: Eerdmans, 1989), 206.

16. Karen Burton Mains, *Making Sunday Special* (Waco: Word, 1987), 25–37.

17. Sara Wenger Shenk, *Why Not Celebrate!* (Intercourse, Pa.: Good Books, 1987), 48–52.

18. *Celtic Daily Prayer*, 87–91.

19. Ibid., 91.

20. Ibid., 87.

21. Dawn, *Keeping the Sabbath Wholly*, 207.

22. Ibid., 2.

23. Ibid., 62.

24. Dorothy C. Bass, *Receiving the Day: Christian Practices for Opening the Gift of Time* (San Francisco: Jossey-Bass, 2000), 77.

Chapter 8 *The Rhythm of Christmas*

1. Matthew Naythons, *Christmas Around the World* (San Francisco: Collins Publisher, 1996), 79.

2. Ibid., 80.

3. L. W. Cowie and John Selwyn, *The Christian Calendar* (Springfield, Mass.: G & C Merriam, 1974), 7.

4. Donna Fletcher Crow, *Seasons of Prayer: Rediscovering Classic Prayers through the Christian Calendar* (Kansas City, Mo.: Beacon Hill, 2000), 9.

5. Robert Webber, *Worship Old and New* (Grand Rapids: Zondervan, 1994), 226.

6. Gertrud Mueller Nelson, *To Dance with God: Family Ritual and Community Celebration* (Mahwah, N.J.: Paulist, 1986), 59.

7. Pat Floyd, *The Special Days and Seasons of the Christian Year* (Nashville: Abingdon, 1998), 6.

8. Crow, *Seasons of Prayer*, 99.

9. Sara Wenger Shenk, *Why Not Celebrate!* (Intercourse, Pa.: Good Books, 1987), 9.

10. Jan Wilson, *Feasting for Festivals* (Oxford: Lion, 1990), 23.

11. C. S. Lewis, *The Lion, the Witch and the Wardrobe* (New York: Penguin, 1959), 23.

12. Joetta Handrich Schlabach, *Extending the Table . . . A World Community Cookbook* (Scottdale, Pa.: Herald, 1991), 202.

13. Dr. Paul Brand with Philip Yancey, *The Gift Nobody Wants* (New York: HarperPerennial, 1993), 13.

14. Shenk, *Why Not Celebrate!* 64.

15. Martha Zimmerman, *Celebrating the Christian Year* (Minneapolis: Bethany, 1994), 65–66.

16. Ibid., 78.

17. "Any Year Calendar—December: Ten Tips for a Simple More Meaningful Christmas" <http://www.simpleliving.org/main/10tips.html> (9 April 2003).

18. Wilson, *Feasting for Festivals*, 18.

19. Nelson, *To Dance with God*, 102.

20. "Treasury of Celebrations: Part 3D: Advent," <http://www.simpleliving.org/Archives/TreasCeleb/TOCAdvent.html> (9 April 2003).

Chapter 9 *Easter: The Rhythm of Healing*

1. Daniel E. Fountain, *God, Medicine, and Miracles* (Wheaton: Harold Shaw, 1999), 220.

2. Brian McLaren, *Finding Faith: A Self-Discovery Guide for Your Spiritual Quest* (Grand Rapids: Zondervan, 1999), 83.

3. Henri Nouwen, Donald McNeill, and Douglas Morrison, *Compassion: A Reflection on the Christian Life* (New York: Image, 1966), 4.

4. Francis McNutt, *Healing* (Notre Dame, Ind.: Ave Maria, 1974), 84.

5. David Bosch, *Transforming Mission* (Maryknoll, N.Y.: Orbis, 1991), 33.

6. Gertrud Mueller Nelson, *To Dance with God: Family Ritual and Community Celebration* (Mahwah, N.J.: Paulist, 1986), 143.

7. Donna Fletcher Crow, *Seasons of Prayer: Rediscovering Classic Prayers through the Christian Calendar* (Kansas City, Mo.: Beacon Hill, 2000), 18.

8. Arlene M. Mark, ed., *Words for Worship* (Scottdale, Pa.: Herald, 1996), 33.

9. Nelson, *To Dance with God*, 139.

10. Judith Newman, "Things that Make You Go 'Ahh,'" *The Oprah Magazine*, October 2002, 252.

11. Alice Dormar, "The Stress Detector Test," *Oprah Magazine*, October 2002, 246.

12. Martha Zimmerman, *Celebrating the Christian Year* (Minneapolis: Bethany, 1994), 115.

13. Ricky Boleman, "Palm Sunday Procession" (Barnes, Wis., Trinity Lutheran Church) <http://www.synodresourcecenter.org/wma/worship/church_seasons/holy_week/palm_sunday/0001/palm_sunday_procession.html> (9 April 2003).

14. Robert Webber, *Rediscovering the Christian Feasts* (Peabody, Mass: Hendrickson, 1998), 66.

15. Visuals of some of the art pieces can be viewed at <http://www.cityside.org.nz>.

16. Zimmerman, *Celebrating the Christian Year*, 149.

17. Evelyn Birge Vitz, *A Continual Feast* (San Francisco: Ignatius, 1985), 211.

Chapter 10 *Rhythm for the Year: Making the Ordinary Extraordinary*

1. Ray Bakke with Jim Hart, *The Urban Christian: Effective Ministry in Today's Urban World* (Downers Grove, Ill.: InterVarsity, 1987), 89.

2. Walter Brueggemann, *Living Toward a Vision: Biblical Reflections on Shalom* (New York: United Church Press, 1976), 16.

3. A Sister of the Society of St. Margaret, *Schools of Spirituality* (West Park, N.Y.: Holy Cross Publications, 1967), 17.

4. For a more comprehensive look at the Rule of St. Benedict, see Joan D. Chittister, *The Rule of Benedict: Insight for the Ages* (New York: Crossroads, 1992).

5. Kathleen Norris, *The Cloister Walk* (New York: Riverside, 1996), 7.

6. Ibid., 8.

7. George Hunter III, *The Celtic Way of Evangelism* (Nashville: Abingdon, 2000), 28.

8. Ibid., 30.

9. For more information, contact Community of Friends in Renewal at icm@icmi.org.

10. Peter Greig, "Holy Monk, Batman," January 2002, <http://www.24-7prayer.com>.

11. For more information, see <http://www.thesimpleway.org>.

12. Esther de Waal gives a full description of the soul friend tradition in *The Celtic Way of Prayer: The Recovery of the Religious Imagination* (New York: Doubleday, 1997), 117–22.

13. Darrell L. Gruder, ed., *Missional Church: A Vision for the Sending of the Church in North America* (Grand Rapids: Eerdmans, 1998), 161.

14. Brueggemann, *Living Toward a Vision*, 51.

15. Paul Brand, *The Forever Feast* (Ann Arbor, Mich.: Vine, 1993), 193–94.

16. Martha Zimmerman, *Celebrate the Feasts of the Old Testament in Your Own Home or Church* (Minneapolis: Bethany, 1981), 171.

17. Christine D. Pohl, *Making Room: Recovering Hospitality as a Christian Tradition* (Grand Rapids: Eerdmans, 1999), 4.

18. Ibid., 6.

19. Ibid., 8.

20. Ibid., 172.

21. Ian Bradley, *Celtic Christian Communities* (Kelowna, B.C.: Northstone, 2000), 12.

22. An ancient Celtic rune from *Guests: In Celebration of Celtic Hospitality* (Norwich, England: Canterbury, 2000), title page.

23. Bradley, *Celtic Christian Communities*, 13.

24. Zimmerman, *Celebrate the Feasts*, 19.

25. Madeleine L'Engle, *Walking on Water: Reflections on Faith and Art* (Wheaton: Harold Shaw, 1980), 52.

26. Ibid., 55.

27. Andrew Rumsey, "The Genius of Creation," *Third Way*, September 1998, 13.

28. Brueggemann, *Living Toward a Vision*, 124.

29. E. Stanley Jones, *The Way* (New York: Abingdon-Cokesbury, 1936), 37.

Christine Sine is an Australian physician who spent twelve years with YWAM as medical director of the Mercy Ships, a ministry that provides medical care and Christian witness in the underdeveloped world. She and her husband, Tom, are consultants for Christian organizations around the world. They are the authors of *Living on Purpose* and founders of Mustard Seed Associates, an international network that encourages Christians to live out their faith. For more information, see their web site, www.msainfo.org. Tom and Christine live in Seattle, Washington.

By CHRISTINE SINE *and* TOM SINE

foreword by Dr. Les Parrott III

Living on Purpose

finding God's best for your life

christine&tomsine

"A practical step-by-step process to create a more focused, less stressed way of life with a difference."
—**Les Parrott**, Ph.D., Center for Relationship Development, Seattle Pacific University

"A must-read for those searching to live life to the max!"
—**Tim Costello**, president, Baptist Union of Australia

"Finally, a practical guide for whole-life stewardship. This book is a compass to navigate one's spiritual gifting and calling in life."
—**Scott Preissler**, president and CEO, Christian Stewardship Association

"If you want to be a part of God turning the world upside down, this book will help you."
—**Paula Harris,** acting director of Urbana, InterVarsity Christian Fellowship

LIVING ON PURPOSE
Finding God's Best for Your Life
0-8010-6388-4

Are you looking for a way of life that is less stressful and more satisfying—a way of life that counts for something? Then begin *Living on Purpose* and discover God's best for your life.

Christine and Tom Sine map out, step-by-step, how you can find and follow God's direction. With this book, you will learn to:

- Make a connection between your Sunday faith and your everyday life seven days a week
- Draft a personal mission statement that will enable you to put first things first
- Reinvent your "timestyle" and lifestyle for a more festive and less driven way of life

See how God can use your life to make a difference in the world. Packed with inspiring true stories and practical, creative direction, *Living on Purpose* will enable you to find a more meaningful and celebrative way of life that truly counts—for today and eternity.